Leadership Skills for Managers

Other titles in the Briefcase Books series include:

Customer Relationship Management by Kristin Anderson and Carol Kerr

Communicating Effectively by Lani Arredondo

Performance Management by Robert Bacal

Manager's Guide to Performance Reviews by Robert Bacal

Recognizing and Rewarding Employees by R. Brayton Bowen

Sales Techniques by Bill Brooks

Motivating Employees by Anne Bruce and James S. Pepitone

Building a High Morale Workplace by Anne Bruce

Six Sigma for Managers by Greg Brue

Design for Six Sigma by Greg Brue and Robert G. Launsby

Negotiating Skills for Managers by Steven P. Cohen

Effective Coaching by Marshall J. Cook

Conflict Resolution by Daniel Dana

Manager's Guide to Strategy by Roger A. Formisano

Project Management by Gary R. Heerkens

Managing Teams by Lawrence Holpp

Budgeting for Managers by Sid Kemp and Eric Dunbar

Hiring Great People by Kevin C. Klinvex, Matthew S. O'Connell, and Christopher P. Klinvex

Time Management by Marc Mancini

Retaining Top Employees by J. Leslie McKeown

Empowering Employees by Kenneth L. Murrell and Mimi Meredith

Presentation Skills for Managers by Jennifer Rotondo and Mike Rotondo, Jr.

Finance for Non-Financial Managers by Gene Siciliano

The Manager's Guide to Business Writing by Suzanne D. Sparks

Skills for New Managers by Morey Stettner

Manager's Survival Guide by Morey Stettner

The Manager's Guide to Effective Meetings by Barbara J. Streibel

Interviewing Techniques for Managers by Carolyn P. Thompson

Managing Multiple Projects by Michael Tobis and Irene P. Tobis

Accounting for Managers by William H. Webster

To learn more about titles in the Briefcase Books series go to
www.briefcasebooks.com

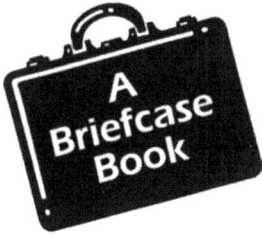

Leadership
Skills for
Managers

Marlene Caroselli

McGraw-Hill

New York San Francisco Washington, D.C. Auckland Bogotá
Caracas Lisbon London Madrid Mexico City Milan
Montreal New Delhi San Juan Singapore
Sydney Tokyo Toronto

ISBN 978-0-07-183175-8

This is a CWL Publishing Enterprises book developed for McGraw-Hill by CWL Publishing Enterprises, Inc., Madison, Wisconsin, www.cwlpub.com.

This publication is designed to provide accurate and authoritative information in regard to the subject matter covered. It is sold with the understanding that neither the author nor the publisher is engaged in rendering legal, accounting, or other professional service. If legal advice or other expert assistance is required, the services of a competent professional person should be sought.
> —*From a Declaration of Principles jointly adopted by a Committee of the American Bar Association and a Committee of Publishers*

McGraw-Hill books are available at special quantity discounts to use as premiums and sales promotions, or for use in corporate training programs. For more information, please write to the Director of Special Sales, McGraw-Hill, 2 Penn Plaza, New York, NY 10121-2298. Or contact your local bookstore.

Contents

Preface   ix

1. **What Is a Leader?**   **1**
   What Is a Manager?   1
   What Is a Leader?   3
   What Traits Do Leaders Exhibit?   4
   Manager's Checklist for Chapter 1   11

2. **The Leader as Visionary**   **13**
   See the Invisible   13
   Welcome Change   14
   Appreciate Vulnerability   16
   Share Knowledge   17
   Attack Complacency   20
   Energize Others   22
   Follow Through   24
   Benchmark   25
   Set Ethical Standards   27
   Assess Yourself   29
   Vision, Courage, Realism, Energy, and Ethics   30
   Manager's Checklist for Chapter 2   31

3. **The Leader as Problem-Solver**   **33**
   Divergent Skills   33
   Convergent Skills   43
   Types of Thinking, Revisited   47
   Manager's Checklist for Chapter 3   48

4. **The Leader as Team-Builder**   **50**
   The Big Picture   50
   Personalities   52

Differing Skills	56
Rewards	58
Conflicts	60
Meetings	62
Keys to Successful Teams	64
Manager's Checklist for Chapter 4	64
5. The Leader as Manager	**66**
Managing Stress	67
Managing Time	72
Managing Emotions	74
Managing Energy	77
Managing People	79
How Much Are You Managing to Manage?	82
Manager's Checklist for Chapter 5	83
6. The Leader as Communicator	**85**
Speaking	85
Motivation	89
Ability to Think on Your Feet	93
Persuasion	98
Writing	100
Manager's Checklist for Chapter 6	101
7. The Leader as Power Distributor	**103**
The Leader's Use of Power	103
Defining Power	104
M-Powers	107
Knowledge Is Power	111
Power Politics	113
Power Struggles	120
Power and Your Potential as a Leader	121
Manager's Checklist for Chapter 7	121
8. The Leader as Liaison	**124**
Fitting the Pieces Together	124
Forming Strategic Alliances	126
The Six C's of Partnering	130
Listening	134
The Trust Factor	135

A Word to the Wise   136
Manager's Checklist for Chapter 8   137

9. The Leader as Planner   138
Long-Range Plans   139
Medium-Range Plans   141
Short-Term Plans   143
Shattering the Myths   143
Planning Tools   145
Things to Remember   147
Manager's Checklist for Chapter 9   152

10. The Leader as ... Leader   154
The Leader Defined   154
The Leader as Visionary   155
The Leader as Problem-Solver   156
The Leader as Team-Builder   157
The Leader as Manager   158
The Leader as Communicator   159
The Leader as Power Distributor   159
The Leader as Liaison   160
The Leader as Planner   160
Your Action Plan   161
The Leader as Leader   162
Manager's Checklist for Chapter 10   162

Index   165

Preface

*L*eadership Skills for Managers is written for the reader who wishes to develop his or her leadership skills. Typically, managers seek such development. In truth, though, anyone can be a leader. Consequently, this book provides a balanced approach: if you want to learn more about management theory, the experts are cited, common wisdom is shared, and best practices are encouraged. And if you want to develop leadership skills, regardless of your place in the organization, tools are presented, examples are given, and first steps are laid out. But if you want to hone both management and leadership skills, the numerous assessments and exercises are designed to enhance your overall competence and to help you move effortlessly into situations that call for one or the other set of skills.

The material in this book should speak to you—in clear, uncomplicated, uncompromising language, the kind of language that leaders employ. The examples should inspire you, the exercises should challenge you, and the information should make you think about the significant responsibilities that leaders assume.

Plan of the Book

The first chapter distinguishes between the functions of leaders and managers, and then goes on to examine the traits typically associated with leadership. The remaining chapters explore the various roles leaders are expected to play and hats they're expected to wear. Among them are the visionary's, the problem-solver's, the team-builder's, and the manager's. In addition, leaders are expected to be outstanding communicators, power-distributors, and liaisons. Finally, they are asked to plan and to learn to integrate the many skills ultimately required to facilitate the success of others.

Special Features of this Book

In addition to assessments, exercises, quizzes, and examples, this book has a unique set of sidebars: smart managing tips, tools, tricks of the trade, definitions, cautions, hints to avoid making mistakes, and examples—all of which illustrate the points being made. Lending depth and richness to the textual tapestry, these special notes will help you absorb and remember the key points made.

Management guru Peter Drucker maintains that "action without thinking is the cause of every failure." Leadership will provoke your thoughts and in so doing will help distance you from failure as you move closer and faster toward success.

Smart Managing

These boxes do just what they say: give you tips and tactics for taking intelligent actions as a leader.

CAUTION!

These boxes provide warnings for where things could go wrong in various situations and how leaders handle such situations.

TRICKS OF THE TRADE

Here you'll find how-to hints to make your leadership actions more effective.

Key Term

Every subject has its special jargon and terms. These boxes provide definitions of these concepts.

For Example

Want to know how others have done it? Look for these boxes.

Here you'll find specific procedures you can follow for special leadership situations.

How can you make sure you won't make a mistake when leading? You can't, but these boxes will give you practical advice on how to minimize the possibility.

Acknowledgments

Alfred Kazin observed that "one writes to make a home for one-self, on paper, in time, in others' minds." Sometimes, this home-making means being mentally absent from the physical home in order to enter the literary one. It means selfishly pursuing ideas and turning away from family members. Writing, after all, is a solitary pursuit, a silent pursuit. The writer cannot engage in conversation while writing, cannot listen to problems, cannot share the loads life puts on shoulders. And so, I acknowledge my indebtedness to my parents, who so stoically and patiently wait-ed for the manuscript to be completed. Now, once again, I can listen to your problems and celebrate your joys.

I also acknowledge my debt to the many corporations, gov-ernment agencies, universities, and associations that have engaged my training and keynoting services. By living in these organizational homes for an hour or a day, I've gleaned so many of the real-world examples that are provided here.

Finally, I wish to thank John Woods of CWL Publishing Enterprises, who exemplifies the wisdom of General Patton's advice: "Give direction, not directions." I am grateful for the freedom he extends to writers, who need to decorate with their own unique flair the interiors of homes they make in others' minds. I also want to thank Bob Magnan of CWL for his editing the final manuscript. We have been a good team.

About the Author

Marlene Caroselli is a prolific writer whose 40 books can be found at Amazon.com or her Web site: http://hometown.aol.com/mccpd. She contributes frequently to Stephen Covey's *Excellence* magazine, Lakewood Publications' sales newsletters, and various other e-columns, sourcebooks, and annuals. In addition, she presents training and keynote addresses for federal and state agencies, corporations, and numerous other organizations. You may reach her at mccpd@aol.com.

What Is a Leader?

Jack Welch, CEO of General Electric, is reported to have called his direct reports together one day. He issued a three-word dictum—"Don't manage! Lead!"—and then promptly left the room. Many were left wondering, "What's the difference?"

That's an important question, so it seems logical that we begin a book on leadership by examining the difference between managing and leading, between a manager and a leader.

What Is a Manager?

The classic definition of a manager is one who gets done through other people. You may be planning, directing, controlling, hiring, delegating, assigning, organizing, motivating, disciplining, or doing any number of other things managers do on a daily basis. No matter what you do, though, you are working toward a goal by helping others do their work.

You are a manager if:

1. **You direct the work, rather than perform it.** Are you frequently tempted to pitch in on a regular basis or to do the work yourself, rather than delegate? If so, you're not spending your time wisely or well. Occasionally, you may have to roll up your sleeves and work with the team on a rush project. Remember, though, you were hired to manage the staff's work—not to be part of the staff.

2. **You have responsibilities for hiring, firing, training, and disciplining employees.** Staff development is an important part of your job. Such development often determines whether staff members stay with an organization or leave for better opportunities. In addition to regular performance appraisals, you should work with each person you manage to determine a career path.

3. **You exercise authority over the quality of work and the conditions under which it is performed**. As a manager, your first obligation is to your people. In part, this obligation means you work to ensure a safe environment for them and to uncover potential threats to that environment. (Does your team know what to do, for example, if all the lights suddenly went out or if a bomb threat were received?) The obligation also means you owe your customers—internal or external—the highest-quality outputs.

4. **You serve as a liaison between employees and upper management.** Managers wear many hats. Among them: traffic cop, psychologist, coach, minister, diplomat, and envoy. In this role, you serve as the link between those doing the work and those who need or benefit from the work being done. The liaison serves as a buffer, a praiser, a translator, and a seeker-of-resources to ensure the work is done more efficiently and the employees are recognized when they've completed it.

5. **You motivate employees and contribute to a culture of accomplishment.** You've no doubt heard that the difference

between ordinary and extraordinary is "that little extra." If you're totally committed to your job as manager, then you're aware of the need to motivate, to instill pride, to create a climate in which innovation can flourish.

> ## Work Smarter   TRICKS OF THE TRADE
>
> Carry a pad and pencil with you for one full day and note every single action you take and how much time it requires. At the end of the day, determine the percentage of time you spent on each activity. Then review the list and put a star next to the activities that helped advance the organizational or departmental mission. Is there a match between important and time-consuming actions? If not, set some new priorities.

What Is a Leader?

While the manager works to carry out the aims of the organization, the leader serves to create new aims, tweak old ones, or initiate new courses of action. Leadership is what Sam Walton was promoting when he encouraged people to "eliminate the dumb." The leader challenges the status quo, in the most positive and diplomatic of ways, in order to continuously improve. It is the leader we turn to when we feel that "good enough" is not.

You are a leader if:

1. **You believe that, working in concert with others, you can make a difference.** It's fairly easy to make money. But leaders strive to make a *difference*. They are willing to make sacrifices and to inspire others to do the same. When John F. Kennedy inspired Americans to give up their life style and join the Peace Corps, he admitted he was asking them to accept the "toughest job you'll ever love."

2. **You create something of value that did not exist before.** When you hear of someone being a leader in a particular field or when you hear of something being the leading edge, you know that person or that thing stands out by virtue of being first or being different. If you can point to one improvement you have implemented in the last six months, you can rightfully call yourself a leader.

3. **You exhibit positive energy.** We gravitate toward individuals who exude confidence. Their magnetism attracts us and we become willing followers. Call it charisma, call it enthusiasm, but know that such individuals easily lead others by virtue of their passion for accomplishment. If you fit this description, then you are known for the way you "attack" various tasks. Your fervor is unbridled. You see hurdles as things to overcome. In short, your energy energizes others.

4. **You actualize.** The true leader goes beyond vision to create a new reality. He* actualizes the dream he has inspired in others. In the process of self-actualizing, the leader is becoming all that he can be and making others believe they can do the same. The leader is committed. He believes the collective actions of the whole team will lead to mission accomplishment.

5. **You welcome change.** Through his commitment to action, the leader treads virgin territory. He spots vacuums and works to fill them. He sees what is invisible and inspires others to make the ideal real. Leaders know that change is progress. And to lessen the fear that progress instills, the leader is out front. He knows that he must take an "I'll go first" approach to convince others that change is not only necessary, but that it can be good.

> **Doubly Dedicated**
> The combination of intellectual and emotional dedication is what coach Vince Lombardi alluded to when he said, "Some guys play with their heads and sure, you need to be smart to be number one in anything you try. But most important, you've got to play with your heart. If you're lucky enough to find a guy with a lot of head and a lot of heart, he'll never come off the field second."

What Traits Do Leaders Exhibit?

Leadership reflects a wide spectrum of traits—all of them admirable, all of them beneficial to others. Because the study of

*For the sake of ease in writing and reading, gender references will be alternated chapter by chapter.

leadership in an ongoing one, there will never be full agreement on what constitutes leadership traits. Nor will students of leadership agree on whether leaders are made or born. Nonetheless, there are certain characteristics that all leaders seem to possess. We'll explore them here.

Obtain Approval CAUTION!

Long-sighted passion has a way of pushing practicality aside. In your rush toward goal attainment, don't overlook conferring with those whose approval you'll need along the way. This includes upper management but also, possibly, customers and other departments that will be impacted by the changes you are proposing.

As we do so, make some mental comparisons. Ask yourself, "To what extent do I possess these qualities?"

Courage

Philosopher Arthur Schopenhauer wisely and wryly observed that "all truth goes through three stages. First it is ridiculed. Then it is violently opposed. Finally, it is accepted as self-evident." Leaders who dare to do something are prepared for opposition. They often take a courageous stand, suggesting that even if something "ain't broke," perhaps it should be fixed nonetheless. Leaders have the courage of their convictions and are ready to be ridiculed, opposed, and ultimately agreed with.

One tool that will help you prepare for the opposition a new idea might engender is called the ABCD Approach. Let's walk through the process. First, think of some way the work environment could be improved. You may want to consider a way to expedite a work process or to improve morale, to develop a new orientation program or to enlist Subject Matter Experts (SME) to conduct some training.

To Avoid Criticism Smart Managing

It's pretty easy to avoid criticism, al least according to philosopher Elbert Hubbard.

Just "do nothing, say nothing, be nothing." Leaders know when their convictions lead them away from conventional thinking, they're bound to hear skeptics complain and ridicule and deride. Only do-nothing people can escape criticism. Surely, you're not one of those.

Whatever your idea is, subject it first to the "A" element: *Anticipate objections*. Ask yourself who is likely to offer what objections to the plan you will propose.

Once you've identified the individuals and the specific negative reactions you're likely to encounter, you can take steps to prepare yourself for the persuading you'll have to do. Cite precedents as part of your persuasion effort. Also arm yourself with statistics to strengthen your position. Finally, garner support—ideally you can quote someone in senior management—and let the resisters know how widespread the approval for your plan actually is.

The "B" aspect of this approach asks you to *"Benefitize"*—i.e., to list all the benefits for various individuals and groups if your project is implemented. The WIIFM Factor ("What's in It for Me?") exerts powerful influence on those you may be trying to win over. Again, whenever possible, cite figures to substantiate the advantages of your proposal.

Many plans never get beyond the planning stage because planners fail to take into account all the individuals and things that might be impacted by the plan, once implemented. The "C" part of the ABCD plan asks you to *Categorize*—to think of all the individuals, departments, groups, schedules, budgets, publicity, locations, etc. that you need to consider and take care of. You should spend as much time on this aspect of initiating a leadership project as you spend on actually developing the project.

Not until you've spent considerable time, energy, and effort on the first three letters of the ABCD Approach should you start the final stage. "D" means *Develop your plans*.

As you do so, don't hesitate to do your homework. Talk to others who may have undertaken an equally ambitious project in the past. Read as much as you can, surf the Net, and subject your plan to the scrutiny of several people whose opinion you respect. Once you've fully developed the plan of action, begin to implement it, assigning to the members of your team the tasks best suited to their individual talents.

Pride

Not only does the leader take pride in his accomplishments, he also creates an atmosphere that allows others to do the same. W. Edwards Deming, one of the founding fathers of the quality movement, asserted that employees are rightfully entitled to the "pride of workmanship." Essential to that pride are job security, expectations, clear communications, and the proper tools.

> ### Leaders Take Pride and Instill Pride
> Smart Managing
>
> Leaders are proud of what they are accomplishing and even more proud of what their followers are accomplishing. Pride does not evolve on its own, however. The leader must take steps to ensure the proper conditions are in place.

How does the leader instill pride? In part, by making followers feel that their efforts are meaningful. In part, by setting the goal and then moving out of the way. (Many leaders subscribe to General George S. Patton's advice: "Give direction, not directions.") Leaders also reinforce expectations, monitor the work being done, set limits of authority and responsibility, and do all they can to help followers get the job done and get it done well.

Here are some of the responsibilities faced by managers who lead. In the blank space before each, write one of these letters to indicate which pride-inducing element is being addressed:

Goal-setting = **G**   Monitor = **M**
Communications = **C**   Tools = **T**

___ Setting deadlines	___ Allocating resources
___ Commending	___ Coaching
___ Measuring outcomes	___ Writing reports
___ Giving instructions	___ Gathering data
___ Providing training	___ Developing standards
___ Aligning task with talent	___ Sharing information

What other responsibilities have you assumed as you worked to instill pride in the work being done? Make a note or two in response to this question and then talk to other managers/leaders who make a determined effort to develop pride.

Sincerity

Leaders show their humanness in several different ways. They manage to convey sincere concern for other people, genuine interest in subjects other than themselves. Given the nature of technology, mega-mergers, and the vastness of customer-supplier networks, it's not always easy for leaders to show a personal touch. Nonetheless, you'll need to find ways to reach out and touch those who are following you and those who are affected by those who are following you.

Your efforts can be as expansive as events planned to celebrate success or as small as a thank-you. But ... they should be ongoing, genuine, and *varied*. (After all, if everyone is "wonderful," no one is wonderful. Your efforts to show appreciation will fizzle if they are repeated too often and/or if they are always the same.)

One of the best ways to demonstrate you truly care about others is help them see in themselves what is so apparent to you. Here's an example to illustrate this point. If you're sending a letter of commendation to someone, send along a folder as well. The folder, labeled "Success" or some other complimentary term, will hold the letter and all such recognitions the person has received in the past and will receive in the future. Suggest that the recipient pull out the folder whenever barriers seem insurmountable. By scanning the recommendations and commendations he's received, the individual cannot help but be energized.

Adaptability

We live not only in a culture of chaos, but also in an age of paradox. We're told to do more with less. We admire "rugged individualists," yet we're expected to be team players. We're encouraged to make elaborate plans and then we're told the future is happening so quickly, it's impossible to plan for it. We learn, over time, that the very skills that enabled us to succeed early on can cause our later failures. We're encouraged to organize but are taught that chaos must reign, if only for a while. We find ourselves agreeing with Sophocles, who noted, "There is a point beyond which even justice becomes unjust."

The leader takes all these contradictions in stride, knowing that the individuals and institutions we revere today can easily wind up in the trash heap of tradition tomorrow. The leader is able to see both sides of the picture, to maintain a balanced perspective like that of Janus, the ancient Roman god. His picture was shown on coins with two profiles: one looked back over the year just ended, the other looked toward the year about to begin. (The month of January is named for Janus.)

To lead is to hold or at least entertain opposing points of view. You've no doubt developed some flexibility by this point in your managerial career so you can consider conflicting ideas. It is safe to say you'll need even more flexibility as computers encourage multi-tasking and multi-thinking at an ever-dizzying pace. Demonstrate your flexibility by taking the suggestions here and in the chapters to follow and adapting them to your own special circumstances.

Information Pressure

You no doubt feel some "information pressure" in your current job. It's the feeling that comes from having too much to read, digest, and learn in too little time. The experts predict that within 10 years, such pressure will be 32 times greater than it is today. Begin now to find ways to streamline intellectual inputs. Filtering your e-mail is one way. Consciously work to find other ways.

Influence

"The key to leadership today," Ken Blanchard maintains, "is influence, not authority." Leaders know how to influence others, to persuade them to a higher calling.

If you intend to lead others, you can't depend on the authority of your managerial position. It can help you, but it can also harm you when trying to reach those who resist "authority figures."

Here are questions designed to help you analyze your influence efforts and to use what you learn to refine your leadership skills.

- Think of the last time you attempted to influence someone. If the effort was successful, what worked? If it wasn't,
  what went wrong?
- When was the last time someone attempted to influence
  you? What evidence was there that he was operating
  with honesty, sincerity, and/or ethical principles?
- To what extent do those who follow you trust you? To
  what extent do you trust them? How can the trust levels
  be raised?
- What words describe the most influential person you
  know? Which of those words could also be applied to
  you?
- Is manipulative behavior ever acceptable? If so, when? If
  not, why not?

Multilingual Abilities

It was Joseph Juran, another giant in the world of quality, who
noted that two languages are spoken in every organization. One
is the "language of things," spoken by nonsupervisory employees. The other is the "language of money," spoken by senior
management. Managers who lead, he asserted, must be bilingual.

Are you able to speak both languages? If not, it may be time
for further training in finance. (An alternative might be to read

⚠ CAUTION!

The Up Side of Manipulation

Be careful about discounting the advantages of manipulative behavior. If you define manipulation as "getting others to do what they might not be inclined to do so we can meet our
own goals," then you'll have to admit you've been manipulating since
you were a baby. (Your parents surely did not want to get up in the
middle of the night to feed you and yet you manipulated them into
doing so.)

Manipulation has a negative connotation only if you're taking advantage of others. When used for neutral or positive reasons, however,
there's nothing wrong with it. For example, when you wear your best
suit to an interview and carry a résumé printed on expensive paper,
you're attempting to influence others to do something they might not
be inclined to do (hire you) so that you can meet your own goals.

Jack Stack's book, *The Great Game of Business* [New York: Bantam Books, 1992]. It spells out, in user-friendly terms, how to make every single employee aware of what he costs and what he contributes to the company.)

And the language of things is not just a single language. More and more, it's necessary for managers to deal with areas of specialization that may each have a different dialect. R & D, production, marketing, sales, shipping and receiving, inventory and supplies, personnel—depending on the organization, these functional divisions can each have a particular culture and language.

You've probably learned by now that the boundaries of your language are the boundaries of your world. If you don't have the words you need to communicate with various specialists in the organization, you'll be banned from their world. You need not become an expert in every field, but you should be conversant so you can converse!

Leadership is always an exciting path to pursue. Leadership in the new millennium, however, is more than an exciting path. It is a colorful highway on which traffic moves at breakneck speed. If you've accepted the challenge of leading in today's business arena, you're clearly a person who goes beyond his managerial role. You have faith in your own courage, pride, sincerity, and adaptability. Further, you know you can influence others, in part because you can speak more than one business language. And now you're eager to progress through the following chapters to develop your leadership abilities.

Manager's Checklist for Chapter 1

❑ Develop both your leadership and your management skills: both are essential to your involvement in running the organization.

❑ Keep a log of your activities so that you can focus better on those that advance the departmental mission.

❑ Establish a culture of accomplishment.

❑ Challenge the status quo: eliminate "the dumb" and create something of value.

❏ Visualize, then actualize.

❏ Demonstrate leadership with an "I'll go first" style.

❏ Obtain approval for changes not just from those above you, but also from those around and below you.

❏ Prepare for opposition. Use the ABCD Approach: Anticipate objections, "Benefitize," Categorize, then Develop the plan.

❏ Praise—but be sure that it's sincere, deserved, and unique.

❏ Reconcile paradoxes for yourself and your followers. They're a fact of life that managers cannot ignore or simplify.

❏ Find ways to avoid being overwhelmed by information.

❏ Develop your influence skills. Don't depend on your authority to get things done.

❏ Assure yourself that manipulation is not always a bad thing. It's only when it's used for exclusive self-gain that it becomes harmful to others.

❏ Make your followers aware of costs, so they understand there's a financial rationale behind most decisions.

The Leader as Visionary

Psychologist Kurt Lewin offers a three-step model for change. If you subscribe to this model, you'll begin by thawing or defrosting the existing situation. You'll recognize the benefits the program or process has afforded in the past, but you'll acknowledge the importance of continuous improvement at the same time. Praise the old while paving the way for the new. Then, when you've created a change-receptive climate, you can introduce the change and then set about stabilizing it. Recognize, though, that even after you have solidified the change and it's become standard operating procedure, in time it too will undergo the thaw-change-refreeze process. It will become an old idea being replaced by a new one.

See the Invisible

Jonathan Swift defined "vision" as the ability to see the invisible. Leaders do just that—they envision a better place, a faster process, a simpler procedure, an improved method of serving customers. They subscribe to the wisdom that asserts, "If it ain't broke, break it!"

Look into the future and make the present road lead there. How? One way is to list 20 things you do in a typical week in performing your job. Experts tell us that five of those need to be streamlined or even eliminated. Let's select just one. Which of those 20 activities or actions could you do without?

Another way to see the invisible is to borrow ideas from other cultures, other fields, other institutions. In fact, about a third of the reading you do should have nothing to do with *what* you do.

Confused? Don't be. This really does make sense. If you're an electrical engineer, for example, you probably read professional journals. Occasionally, you should read articles that have nothing to do with electrical engineering. Often, ideas are born by exposure to the new and different. These ideas can then be applied to enhance the work we actually do.

This is why Peter Drucker, known as the father of modern management science, once gave this advice to a young manager seeking to excel in his field: "Learn to play the violin." As strange as it initially seems, the skills of discipline and listening and harmonizing with others all relate to the art and science of management.

You can also glean ideas for improving present circumstances by developing a vision based upon your knowledge of current events.

Welcome Change

In the Finnish language, "management" and "leadership" are not separate terms. One word covers both concepts. In America, the fact that there are two words suggests there are two different functions. Can someone be an excellent manager without being a leader? Can someone be an outstanding leader without being a manager? The answer to both questions is "yes," especially if you agree with the definitions cited earlier: managers maintain the status quo while leaders alter it.

To be sure, you can alter it by degrees. You need not take the extreme approach advocated by musician Miles Davis:

"Never do today what you did yesterday." But you should take the approach advocated by Sam Walton, who encouraged his employees at Wal-Mart to "eliminate the dumb."

No matter how proficient your work environment is, no matter how productive your coworkers are, there's always room for improvement. Some of the steps you're taking to execute certain processes are unnecessary. Just look around you. You're bound to find ways to eliminate ... if not the absurd, then at least the wasteful, the time-consuming, the overly expensive cost of doing business.

You can regard change reactively or proactively. Of the two, the latter is easier. Rather than have change foisted upon you, you can lead the change. There are certain qualities change agents possess. Assess yourself by answering "yes" or "no" to the following questions.

> ### Don't Deny You're in Denial
>
> You can doom your own career—and organizations can doom their own future—if you deny the need for change. No matter how successful you are, if you're not responding to the opportunities born of rapid change in the larger society, you're allowing others in the fast lane to overtake you. Change, says Alan Cohen, management professor at Babson College, "is the antithesis of denial." Stop denying that things could be better. Take a risk. Remember that yes-men and yes-women typically go nowhere.

Change Assessment

	Yes	No
1. I tell the truth, as gently as possible, about what I think is wrong.	___	___
2. I encourage questions.	___	___
3. I am effective at persuading others.	___	___
4. I realize change is loss and people need to grieve losses.	___	___
5. I regard myself as a continuous learner.	___	___
6. I regard myself as a realist.	___	___
7. I believe in a highly formalized planning.	___	___
8. I am comfortable with temporary chaos.	___	___

	Yes	No
9. I am certain I know what our customers want.	___	___
10. I am more interested in content than appearance.	___	___

Scoring: The more "yes" answers you had (with two exceptions), the more likely you are to initiate change, help others engage in the change process, and enjoy the consequences.

Question #7 is one to which, ideally, you answered "no." The more formalized the planning sessions in your organization, the greater the deniability factor. That is, the discontent or concerns of lower-echelon employees are not likely to penetrate the layers that surround and protect the upper-echelon ranks.

A rigidity about customer relations (Question #9) can actually lead to customer loss. Even if you do know what your customers want today, their needs may change tomorrow. You should have some uncertainly regarding your customers' desires.

If you did well on this assessment, you probably believe in the wisdom of the old saw, "If you always do what you've always done, you'll always get what you've already got. You'll always be what you already are."

Appreciate Vulnerability

An uncommon view of leadership is espoused by Howard Schultz, CEO of Starbucks. "The leader," he asserts, "has to display vulnerability." Do you agree or disagree with his pronouncement?

Before you answer, consider another view of the question. *Fast Company* magazine interviewed Richard Russell ("Navigating Change" by Anna Muoio, May 1999, page 76), who directs corporate strategy development for the Naval Undersea Warfare Center in Newport, Rhode Island. "We used to have a clear set of rules, a clear understanding of the threat that we faced," he observes. "Now we've got a new set of vulnerabilities—which means that we have to think differently."

Being able to recognize vulnerabilities is a critical trait for leaders. So is being able to honestly acknowledge their existence to others. A third valuable trait is being able to think of new approaches to strengthen the weak spots in the organizational structure.

> **Drucker, Again**
>
> Peter Drucker asserts, "Leaders know how to ask questions—the right questions."
>
> Rather than accepting the current state of affairs, leaders continuously challenge. They poke, they prod, they probe beneath the coating that inevitably forms on the milk of human activity. Think about the questions you've asked this week. Would others regard them as the type of questions leaders ask?
>
> *Smart Managing*

As we've noted before, leaders don't hesitate to join disparate elements. John F. Kennedy, for example, was famous for bringing to cabinet meetings individuals from various walks of life. Similarly, Richard Russell convenes people from different professions and asks them questions that are "bold, daring, and different." Among those tough questions is one he asks of his employees, "Why do we exist?"

Answering this question alone will lead to discussion and affirmation of core values. It will help people to put aside petty diversions and concentrate on the true mission. The person who complains, for example, that phone calls interrupt his work needs to be reminded that phone calls *are* his work. Those who are less than gracious in their attitude toward customers need to be reminded that without customers, they'd be without a job. These questions help set the mission compass toward north again.

Share Knowledge

A buzzword has emerged to describe the practice of excluding others in terms of knowledge: "silo-ism." There are those—no doubt

> **Silo-ism** The selfish practice of keeping work-related knowledge to oneself in order to prevent others from working as efficiently as possible. People who engage in this practice are typically power-hungry. They attempt to build their own power base but in the process destroy any trust their coworkers could have in them.
>
> *Key Term*

you've met a few in your career—who believe knowledge is power, and the more knowledge they can acquire for themselves, the more powerful they will be. They build metaphorical silos around themselves—keeping knowledge in and people out.

Are You Sharing Knowledge?

By contrast, effective leaders share knowledge. They know the importance of keeping the cadre of followers informed. "The best strategy for the future," author Nancy Austin declares, "is wholesale, wall-to-wall information sharing."

How extensive is your own process of sharing information? Take this quiz to find out. Read the statements. Then decide which of them best describes your relationship to knowledge and to the people who need it. (More than one may apply.)

___ Have knowledge
___ Have and share knowledge
___ Don't have
___ Don't have but would share if I did
___ Don't have and would not share if I did
___ Can't get it and wouldn't share it if I could
___ Can't get it but would share it if I could
___ Know who needs it
___ Know who wants it

Ask your team members to assess you, if you're brave, in terms of these attributes. Ask your boss, if you're even braver, if the two of you can discuss the way he or she makes use of knowledge, according to the descriptions above.

Are You Involving Others?

When you have to think fast and act fast, you often do so without involving others. In times of true crisis, such response is critical. However, most of the decisions you make don't border on the critical. Are you making those decisions by yourself most of the time? If so, what prompts such behavior? Is it the need to save time? Is it just your style? Is it a matter of thinking you have the best answers or the best information?

Consider the following questions. They may guide you toward greater inclusion and power-sharing in actions to take in the future.

Think about the last important decision you made. On a scale of 1-10 (low to high), what was the urgency surrounding the decision? (In other words, if you had to react quickly, you would rate the urgency factor high.)

Now list those who were affected by that decision:

Person A: _____

Person B: _____

Person C: _____

Which of these persons did you consult before you made the decision? _____

Which of these persons provided information that influenced your decision? _____

Which of these persons did you meet with after you made the decision? _____

If you had to make the same (or a similar) urgent decision again, would you change your decision-making strategy in view of these questions? Explain why or why not.

Are You Using the Best Medium?

This is a true story. In a well-known aerospace firm, in the pre-computer days, an elderly secretary found she was having some difficulty reading the handwriting of the engineers for whom she typed reports. She confided in the department manager, whom she had known for many years, and asked for his help. Had you been that manager, what would you have done?

If you opted to speak to your team at the next staff meeting, your request would have sounded something like this: "Before we start today's meeting, I'd like to point out that Ellie is having some trouble reading your handwriting. Please, either print or skip every other line to make it easier for her." It takes about eight seconds to say these words.

Instead, the manager chose to put the request in writing. The one-and-a-half-page memo—which had to be typed by Ellie, copied, stapled, delivered to 23 engineers, and read by 23 engineers—began with these words: "Due to the vagaries and idiosyncratic differences in the individual handwritten styles of the members of this department, it is incumbent upon me at this time to advise you that . . . ."

Seek Feedback

From time to time, ask your team members how they felt about a recent communication. Was it clear? Did it come at the right time? Was the tone appropriate? Were all the people who needed the information included? The unexamined life, we know from the ancient Greeks, is not worth living. By extension, the unexamined management style is not worth being proud of.

It's not enough to decide to share information. You also have to decide the best time, place, and medium for that communication. Technology has broadened the array of available choices but you still must use good judgment to determine what works best for whom at what time.

Attack Complacency

Reliving past successes produces feel-good emotions. Such emotions are important for maintaining interest and momentum. If you *rest* on your laurels, however, you cannot advance the action.

Leaders attack complacency. They challenge themselves and others to better their personal best. They bring an intensity to their work. They know good enough seldom is.

From the world spanned by golden arches comes a good example of competing against yourself. McDonald's engages in corporate introspection. Ed Rensi, a high-ranking executive with the firm, spends several days a week visiting the various locations. As he "walks the walk and talks the talk," he learns what's important to employees. He also learns what's important to customers, rewarding them with free food in exchange for their honest opinions.

You can do the same. Attack the complacency that feel-good moments can breed by inviting opinions from those directly and indirectly involved with the work you do. The invitation can be formal or informal, oral or written, directed to small groups or large.

> ### It's More than a Game
> A good example of the drive toward excellence can be found in Jack Lambert, former Pittsburgh Steeler linebacker. He had strong feelings about the competition and used those feelings to spur himself to win. "If we lose," he once revealed, "it could affect my livelihood. It's not just a game to me."

When Motorola opened its semiconductor facility in Kuala Lumpur in the early '90s, it also began a program to improve productivity. This "I recommend" program encouraged ideas from employees. In return, management promised a reply within three days. The first year found the work force of 5,000 making 8,000 recommendations. The next year, that number doubled. Imagine how your organization could benefit if each employee were averaging three ideas a year or more! Of course, such programs work only if *you* are working: if the ideas are floating into a bureaucratic black hole, employees will soon lose faith in your leadership.

Staff meetings provide another way to motivate others to ongoing achievement. Before your next meeting begins, ask your team, "What do we need to do better?" Award a token prize to the person with the longest list. Then discuss the discrepancies between team members' perspectives and your own.

Complacent or Challenged?

Look at the words in the columns on the next page and encircle those that describe your actions at least half the time. If there are some that describe you 100% of the time, draw a box around those descriptors. (Note: You may want to make a copy of this list before marking on it.)

skeptical	rushed	accommodating
authentic	empathetic	social
demanding	disciplined	firm
organized	vulnerable	witty
self-starting	knowledgeable	creative
visionary	supportive	cautious
verbal	tolerant	collaborative
gracious	definite	efficient
defensive	resourceful	process-oriented
analytical	inspired	driven
intuitive	flexible	impartial
forgiving	loyal	entrepreneurial
stressed	materialistic	confident
political	decisive	cooperative

Analysis: For those you've drawn a box around, consider how those traits relate to the complacency and/or the challenges with which you regard your job. Think about this long and hard. It's the only way to find out if attitude adjustments are called for. If you are truly interested in learning more about how others perceive you, have your subordinates assess you in the same way. Then discuss their perceptions—especially where they differ from your own.

Energize Others

You have achieved excellence as a leader, according to Colin Powell, "if people will follow you anywhere—if only out of curiosity." If you serve as an organizational magnet, it is probably because others find you optimistic, energetic, idealistic, and/or fun to be around. One way to assess your optimism is to list all the barriers to excellence within the workplace (aim for 20 at least). Make your list now and—if you want to bring out energy and idealism in others while having fun at the same time—work with your team on this exercise.

Once you have the list, go back and write the letter "C" in front of those items over which you can exert partial or complete control. Afterwards, assess yourself. If you possess the energizing battery, you will have written a "C" in front of half the items—at least. If you've C'd only a few items, go back and reconsider ways you can empower yourself and others to take ownership of the things that matter.

> ### Don't Downsize the Downsides
> **TOOLS**
>
> Before you begin to energize others for your next leadership project, follow the recommendation of Andrew Campbell and Michael Goold (*The Collaborative Enterprise*, New York: Perseus Press, 1999): for every upside or advantage that can result from the successful implementation of your idea, identify a downside. Address it and be prepared to deal with it if and when it arises.

If you have an energizing personality, you probably believe in synergy. You understand how the total outcome can be greater than the sum of its parts. But if you've not yet discovered the power of working as a unit, try this little experiment. Set your timer for 10 minutes first. Now, without looking at anything except a blank piece of paper, write all the works you can think of that begin with the letter "m." When the timer goes off, stop.

The second part of the experiment asks you to assemble 10 people. Set the timer this time for only one minute. Ask them to write as many words that begin with the letter "m" as they possibly can within one minute. When the timer goes off,

> ### Are You More Like Revere or Like Dawes?
> **Smart Managing**
>
> Chances are you know about Paul Revere and his midnight ride. But did you know there was another rider who also alerted the townsfolk of New England late one April night, 225 years ago? The second rider was William Dawes, who took the southern route while Revere headed north. History barely remembers Dawes because the townspeople barely noticed him. Unlike Revere, who energized all those he encountered, Dawes was so softspoken that he failed to rally others around the cause.
>
> Think of the last time you aroused interest at work, the last time you rallied others in support of an idea or cause you believed in. Keep that memory fresh in your mind the next time you choose to lead a leadership project.

ask them to eliminate duplicate words and then see what the total is. Chances are it will be greater than the number you found working alone for the same number of total minutes.

Follow Through

The leaders we willingly follow tell us what they'll do and then they do what they said they would. Are you such a leader? Do others trust your word? Can you execute the details necessary to move your vision from the ideal to the real?

Thousands of years ago, Chinese philosopher Lao-tzu gave this nutshell definition of leadership: "To lead the people, walk behind them." With these few words, he stresses the importance of trusting and supporting your followers. You don't always have to lead the parade. Sometimes you can bring up the rear. Leaders who trust and respect their followers don't micromanage them. Nontrusting managers look over their employees' shoulders, trying to ensure the work is carried out exactly as they think it should be.

Trusting managers have faith in the competencies of their followers. They know details will be attended to. What's more, they know employees will take care of details in ways they themselves would not even have considered.

When leaders follow through, they monitor the work they've empowered others to do—not every minute of the day but instead with periodic progress checks. Managers who assume empowerment means "power to the people" have a responsibility to explain how the people should use that power. Empty phrases such as "do whatever it takes" leave employees wondering exactly what they're supposed to do.

Managers operating in a leadership mode encourage their subordinates to take initial small steps, then greater steps toward autonomy. They trust employees will not "give away the store." And employees trust they are not regarded as "inmates" to whom the "asylum" has been turned over.

To ensure nothing falls through the cracks created by the divide of power, you can work through details with employees. Ask questions such as:

- Who has responsibility for what?
- What are the deadlines?
- What are the spending limits?
- What outputs are expected?

Benchmark

Benchmarking is a bandwagon on which most organizations have climbed. Simply put, the process helps individuals and organizations improve by measuring their performance against the performance of exemplars. They then use those comparisons as the stimulus for new strategies that can improve performance.

Leaders are realists—they know whatever problem they're facing, someone else in America has already faced it and probably solved it! Whatever aspect of the workplace they would like to improve, they vow to find someone else who's already achieved that goal. Whatever issue needs to be resolved, someone somewhere has likely achieved a satisfactory resolution. Don't get us wrong, here. We're not saying there is no room for innovative thought. But in broad brush strokes—whether the issues are productivity, morale, stress, customers—you can learn from the work of others.

You *can't* learn, though, if you're not reaching out. Benchmark as often as you can. It's an excellent way to make the comparisons necessary for having others join, as the Lexus ads put it, "the relentless quest for perfection."

It's Not Sarcasm, Really!

When you think about assembling a benchmarking team, ask yourself these two questions, which will sound sarcastic at first, but really are not: "Who knows?" and "Who cares?"

You'll want at least one person on your team who is knowledgable about the process you are trying to streamline. You'll also want someone who cares deeply about the process being studied.

Follow These Steps

Benchmarking can be an informal process or a highly formal one. In the interest of time, we recommend the informal approach and a small improvement project. If the efforts pay off, then you can undertake a larger, more formal approach.

1. Begin by defining the problem or the condition you'd like to improve.
2. Next, decide what other organization represents the ideal as far as this particular situation is concerned. Don't limit yourself to companies in your own field. If you like the spirit of creativity that exists at Apple or the joy-inspiring efforts under way at Ben & Jerry's, if you admire the customer-orientation of Xerox or the efficiency of a dot-com organization, let them be your guide.
3. Assemble a team of eight or nine people. (Note: if your benchmarking plans include actually visiting the exemplar's site, send only four people. The whole team could prove to be disruptive for both the benchmarkers and the benchmarkees.)
4. Determine with your team the scope of your project. What specific outcomes are you hoping to achieve? How much time/money can you afford to spend on this project? Who will the results be shared with? Does upper management agree with the importance of the issue you've chosen to study? Do you want to study specific steps in a process or the process itself? These and other questions should be carefully explored prior to launching your benchmarking effort.
5. Select the means by which data will be acquired. Site visits are one way. Reading books and magazines is another. Searching the Internet a third. Telephone and e-mail exchanges are yet another. Employing the services of a benchmarking clearinghouse (such as the American Productivity & Quality Center's International Benchmarking Clearinghouse) is an alternative as well. Assign team members specific tasks and mediums.
6. Synthesize the results of the team members' new knowledge. Discuss at great length the possibilities most applicable to your own situation.

7. Develop an action proposal, to be shared with all those who will be affected by the new process and also with those whose approval is necessary.
8. Implement the plan, with monitoring and adjustments as needed.

Set Ethical Standards

Leaders understand power. They regard it as a means to achieve ethical ends. Used in this way, power leads to win/win/win results.

Typically, we think in win/win terms. You win and I win. But win/win/win encourages a broader range of winners. Leaders add the third component, an additional person, group, or institution that will benefit from the "wins" of the first two parties. The third winner might be the organization or customers or the industry.

As a manager who leads, it's your job to communicate the ethical standards by which your leadership plans will be executed. You can, and probably should, formulate a set of guidelines, such as those developed in 1932 by businessman Herbert J. Taylor. To evaluate the worth of intended actions, he asked:

- Is it the truth?
- Is it fair to all concerned?
- Will it build goodwill and better friendships?
- Will it be beneficial to all concerned?

Principled Persuasion (Rochester, NY: CPD Press, 1999, pp. 338-340) lists other questions that will help you formulate the guidelines for directing the ethical actions of your team. Without such standards, the mission—even if it's accomplished—becomes suspect. If you and/or your followers act in unethical ways, the entire process becomes suspect and the mission is tainted. The unethical behavior may not even be directly related to the work you are doing, but once it's uncovered, it will tarnish your reputation and the goodwill originally generated by the mission and your zeal.

Questions like the following will help resolve the ethical issues that often arise in pursuit of a goal.

- Could this action harm us in any way?
- Could it harm others?
- Is it legal?
- Does it feel wrong?
- If the customer could see us doing this, would she be willing to pay for it?
- Would I still do this if it appeared as a front-page head-line in tomorrow's paper?
- Would we be proud to do this with our families watching?
- Who will be the primary beneficiary of this action? The secondary beneficiary?
- Are there safety/union/OSHA issues we may have over-looked?
- What actions would constitute violations of ethical conduct?
- What are the consequences of such violations?
- In what ways might we be, even unknowingly, pressuring others to act unethically?
- How can we maintain quality when we have to do more with less?
- In different circumstances (i.e., transculturally), how might tolerance limits shift?
- Should we create a hot line or an ombudsman position?
- How and how often should our ethical stance be dissemi-nated?
- What complex or confusing situations might make this stance seem murky to some?
- What could cause confidence to be shaken?
- Does this action advance our mission?
- Is it in keeping with our values?
- Would we be proud to say afterwards that we were a part of this action?
- What assurances could we give regarding possible out-comes?
- Could we be rewarding unethical behavior in any way?
- What could we point to in the past that shows we have an ethical track record?

Leadership "The use of power to effect positive change"— that's how we've defined it. "Power," in and of itself, is not a negative term. Like "leadership," it's a neutral term. Yes, it can be abused, but it can also be used for the common good. All the other words we associate with leadership can be related to these key words: "positive change."

The same is true of "influence." By itself, the term is neutral. Used for negative purposes, it falls outside our definition. Used for positive reasons, it's an attribute shared by leaders.

There is no doubt Hitler was a leader, but not according to our terms. Along the same lines, there is no doubt Jim Jones had tremendous influence powers—proven by his ability to convince 900 people to commit suicide. But these individuals are not ones we admire. Consequently, we can't consider them leaders or influencers whom we want to emulate.

- What ethical messages are we sending or failing to send to others?
- Do people know what to do or whom to turn to if they have ethical concerns?
- If we could develop an intranet message about integrity, what would it say?

Assess Yourself

There are as many ways to assess your leadership as there are qualities associated with it. One of our favorites is based on the work of David McClelland of Harvard. His use of thematic apperception tests is widely applied to the workplace. A sample is included here.

As you study this figure, "Thematic Apperception Test," decide which one of the following scenarios comes closest to what you think is happening here.

1. This person is a well-known lecturer, who has been hired to tell employees about the damaging effects of stress.
2. This person is part of the social events team and is laying out plans for the next get-together.
3. This person is using charismatic power to get others to jump on his bandwagon.
4. This person has been appointed to head a project to cut costs.
5. This person is planning a company-sponsored softball game.
6. This person is a consultant, teaching others how to create intranets.

McClelland found that people are motivated by one of three strong drives to do the best work of which they are capable. We all have some of these drives operative: the need for achievement, the need for power, the need for affiliation. But managers with the strongest power drive make the best managers. They are comfortable with the use of power. They are not so interested in personal accomplishment as accomplishment via coordinating the talents of others. The one answer that suggests both the need for power and the vision leaders must have is answer #3.

If you didn't select it, it doesn't mean you don't have leadership potential. This was, after all, a simplified version of the extensive apperception testing done to find out what kind of work employees are best suited to. Given a series of tests, you might have scored quite differently.

But if you did choose #3, this suggests you already have some of the characteristics we associate with effective leaders.

Vision, Courage, Realism, Energy, and Ethics

For leaders to effect positive change, they must have a picture of what the improvement will look like. That improvement, on a small or grand scale, is called a vision. (Both types are possible, despite opposing views of scale. Mother Teresa, for example, asserted, "We can do no great things..., only small things with great love." By contrast, an anonymous sage urged, "Make no small plans, for small plans have no power to stir the soul.")

Leaders need more than a vision, however. They need to face change with courage and to assure others the future will be better than the present. They need to acknowledge vulnerability—both personal and organizational—rather than pretend or gloss over possible danger. Further, leaders have to share knowledge so others can read from the same, complete metaphorical sheet of music.

While leaders point with pride to past accomplishment, they're not content to remain in the current pride position for long. Energizing others around their new and improved vision, leaders work to create a new reality. They monitor results so details are attended to and benchmark with exemplars so industry-best practices can be adopted and adapted. They do all of this within an ethical context.

Manager's Checklist for Chapter 2

❏ Actively employ your imagination to visualize improvements in place.

❏ Work continuously to streamline your work.

❏ Read outside your field.

❏ Stop denying the need for change.

❏ Take appropriate risks.

❏ Don't assume you completely understand your customers' needs.

❏ Consider the question of vulnerability as it relates to leadership.

❏ Make sure you're asking questions—the right questions.

❏ Share knowledge and involve others as needed.

❏ Think carefully about what needs to be put in writing.

❏ Ask followers, on occasion, for feedback about your communications.

❑ Encourage suggestions from employees.

❑ Strive for energy, idealism, and fun in your leadership overtures.

❑ Address the downside of your ideas.

❑ Remove barriers.

❑ Avoid micromanaging.

❑ Follow through on your promises. Deliver more than you promise.

❑ Encourage your subordinates to take ever larger steps toward independence.

❑ Benchmark to find solutions to common problems.

❑ Aim for win/win/win outcomes.

❑ Establish ethical guidelines.

❑ Develop comfort in the use of power.

3

The Leader as Problem-Solver

Leaders need both divergent and convergent skills to resolve the problems that arise when they try to actualize their vision. If you're dependent upon a certain set of skills—say the logical type—you may have difficulty solving problems that call for innovative thought. The reverse is true as well: if you pride yourself on your creative abilities, you may not be employing analytical skills when they're called for.

Divergent Skills

People who think divergently don't give typical responses. They give atypical ones. An example of a *convergent* reply would be the person who says, "Four" when asked, "How much are two and two?" A *divergent* thinker, asked the same question, might reply, "That's how many people I have coming to dinner so I have to leave work early today."

Divergent thinking is especially useful when you encounter problems without precedent or problems for which precedents are no longer working. Too, some "problems" aren't problems

> ### Movers and (Hand) Shakers
>
> Here's the problem. There are eight managers in a room. Each one shakes hands just once with each of the other managers. What is the total number of handshakes? Now if you are inclined toward algebraic equations, you'd know that you can solve the problem by multiplying the number (eight) by the number minus one (seven) and then dividing that total (56) in half, yielding the correct answer: 28.
>
> But if your math skills were sluggish on a particular day and you had other problem-solving skills, such as visualization, you might draw a series of circles to represent the eight managers, and then start drawing arrows to represent each set of handshakes. You'd arrive at the same answer.
>
> A third possibility is one that physically active people would employ. If you're this type of hands-on problem-solver, you'd gather seven other people around you and begin the actual process of handshaking until you reached the logical conclusion and the correct answer.

at all but rather situations or practices a "problem-solver" would like to make better.

Divergent thinkers refuse to be confined to the boxes in which our jobs typically place us. They know they are capable of new and interesting thoughts; they believe the scientists who tell us we are using only 1% to 10% of the brainpower with which we've been endowed.

Deviate

To lead others toward your vision, that vision must be so different from the existing condition that the difference actually tempts us. Don't hesitate to deviate from known and well-traveled paths. Be a trailblazer in the land of ideas.

Juxtapose Disparate Elements. One easy way to develop new ideas is to juxtapose disparate elements and then try to find connections among them—connections that could relate to a problem you are facing. For example, look at the list of unrelated words following the problem described in the following italicized passage. Then circle two that are sparking ideas for you—ideas that could lead to a new approach for solving the problem.

One member of the team is frequently late to meetings, seldom volunteers to take on responsibility, and, when she does, turns in work that is only marginally acceptable.

tiger	eleven	tears	ear	sweets	target
glue	book	jester	calendar	spirit	balance
memory	ostrich	monolog	delinquent	tooth	butterfly
insight	surgery	newspaper	rose	wonder	gloves
moonlight	ocean	nail	purse	mop	staple

Here's how juxtaposing works. Let's say you chose "calendar" and "surgery."

The first word makes you think of progress reports. You can actually see yourself writing a note to yourself on your calendar, reminding you to ask this team member how much progress she's made on her assignment and offering to assist in some small way if she's not even started. (This is, generally speaking, a good management technique: don't wait until the last minute to verify expectations. It may be too late then. Instead, be ready to discuss milestone dates when you check in and check out.)

The second word, "surgery," makes you think of going beneath the surface. Perhaps you realize that you typically don't go "beneath the surface" to learn what the core problem is. The individual may be having some personal problems that are preventing her from doing as well as she ordinarily does. Or she may be on medication that causes her to be less efficient than usual. She may even be thinking about resigning or retiring—factors that can contribute to her attitude toward her work.

> ## Don't Be a Victim of Your Culture
>
> Author Samuel I. Hayakawa once observed that "if you see in any given situation only what everybody else can see, you can be said to be so much a representative of your culture that you are a victim of it." To be sure, there are boundaries you cannot cross at work—but there are uncountable ones you *can* cross. When's the last time you saw something nobody else had seen and did something about it?

What two words did you choose? What new approaches did they lead you to?

Play a Different Role. When Dr. Jonas Salk was asked by reporters what led him to the discovery of the polio vaccine, he surprised them with his answer: "I learned to think like Mother Nature." If you're not afraid to deviate from tried, true, and tested approaches, you might try looking at a given problem from the perspective of Mother Nature or Father Time, a minister or a child, a surgeon or a nun, etc. For the manager to whom others turn when they need leadership and/or guidance, such perspective shifts are valuable tools.

Personify the Problem. From the world of psychology comes the term "autonomy of object." Essentially, it means regarding the problem as if it were a person, but a person living in a different time, a different place. To illustrate, let's assume the problem is rumor-spreading at work. Now imagine that problem as an actual person, walking around in … Paris between the two world wars. Rumor-Spreading lives, breathes, and strolls along the Champs Elysées. Imagine your problem doing that. What else do you see?

Well, if you're familiar with the American expatriates who lived there then, you might see Ernest Hemingway having a drink with Rumor-Spreading at Harry's Bar. Or you might envision him watching Picasso painting misplaced eyeballs. Or you might see Rumor-Spreading deep in conversation with Gertrude Stein. From this collection of images, you can derive ideas for solving this problem.

The image of Hemingway, with his macho approach to life, could encourage you to tackle the problem head on—perhaps by honestly and directly dealing with the person who is doing the spreading. Maybe the distortions painted by Picasso would lead you to a counter campaign in which you out-rumored the rumors. Stein might inspire you to create a statement and post it everywhere. You'll come up with something more memorable than "a rose is a rose," we're confident.

Incubate

Author Norman Mailer once remarked, "There's this faculty in the human mind that hates any question that takes more than ten seconds to answer." We Americans tend to lead both our personal and professional lives in the fast lane. We think quickly, decide quickly, and move quickly. When problem-solving, though, we have to slow down a bit

> ### The Range of Requisite Behaviors
>
> Smart Managing
>
> This term comes from the animal kingdom, where the animals with the most extensive range of skills for adapting are the animals that survive. There are dozens of valuable problem-solving tools. Continue to add them to your leadership tool kit. The greater your range of requisite behaviors, the more choices you'll have when faced with the problems we expect leaders to solve.

Not all problems have to be solved "on the spot." Nor should they be. Some problems deserve the time needed to percolate in the coffeepot of creativity, to bounce around the mental gymnasiums, to ferment in the vats of invention. You'll find creative people indulge themselves by letting ideas incubate.

Make Lists Now. A simple method of giving potential problems incubation time simply requires you to make a list of at least 25 corporate trouble spots. Ask a dozen people what serious problems will emerge in the next five years. Eliminate duplicates and prepare a prioritized list. Revisit that list every three months with your staff. Ask if the priorities have changed. More important, ask what solutions come to mind for the most serious of these problems. Make note of the suggestions and discuss their viability at the next staff meeting, at which you'll engage in the same process of reprioritizing and noting possible solutions.

Turn to the Outside World. General Electric's CEO, Jack Welch, once warned his staff: "If the rate of change *outside* the organization is greater than the rate of change *inside* the organization, then we are looking at the beginning of the end."

Where to find out what's changing outside the organization? Just study the headlines on any given day. Make note of trends,

Approbation and Probation

Once the gestation period is over and your idea is ready to emerge, you can help it survive in two ways. The first is approbation. Get official approval before investing time and energy in carrying out your leadership project. Few things are more frustrating for followers than to invest energy in a project that excites them, only to learn it didn't pass the approval test.

Second, if you anticipate resistance from significant organizational others, suggest the idea go "on probation." In other words, you're not asking for complete endorsement. Rather, you'd just like a chance to test the idea out. If it proves to be as valuable as you think it will, then you can ask for total support.

technological advances, opinion polls, political movements, world issues, etc. The Oklahoma City bombing, for example, should have prompted the preparation of evacuation plans if they didn't already exist. News about violence in the workplace should have leaders thinking about training or counseling programs or other safety measures.

Again, your records serve as gestation locations for ideas yet to be born. Armed with those ideas, you can put your leadership skills to work.

Obviate

The word "leader" has many connotations. Among them is the concept of an "idea-warrior."

You have to be such a person sometimes. You have to fight for your ideas. This may mean persuading others to give those ideas a chance. You have to obviate the "idea-toxins" before they can strangle your concept struggling to be born.

We've all heard the killer phrases: "It'll never work." "What a dumb idea." "Management would never approve it." If you permit such negativity to poison your innovative thoughts, they'll never have a chance. Instead, you have to counter the effects of such offensives with a strong defense. Here are some ways to do that.

Refer to a Higher Authority. Leaders employ a number of persuasion techniques. One of the most successful is to cite a higher authority. If, for example, your manager is downplaying the need for a writing skills class, you might point out that President Clinton issued a directive calling for the use of plain English in government documents. Citing the President's directive that calls for simple language will make your argument more convincing.

Of course, if you can quote a highly revered executive in your own organization, you might earn even greater credence for your ideas.

Convert the Criticism to a Question. One easy technique for deflecting criticism is to take the negative statement and shape it into a question. For example, if someone tells you, "We've already tried that. It didn't work then and it won't work now," you could reply, "But *why* didn't it work then, George? Wasn't it because we weren't online at the time? Things are different now. We're fully automated and I think the idea *will* work now."

Cite Precedent. A little bit of homework can result in a big payoff for you. If you can cite precedents in other divisions, for example, then you can undermine your opposition very easily. The battle for acceptance has probably already been fought and won in some other places. Referring to that acceptance paves the way for your own idea to thrive.

Cite Statistics. There are those for whom the bottom line is the top of the line, in terms of their receptivity to new ideas. With people of this persuasion, gather your facts and figures and let them speak for you.

Use an Anecdote. There is some interesting research by Joanne Martin and Melanie E. Powers ("Organizational Stories: More Vivid and Persuasive than Quantitative Data," in *Psychological Foundations of Organizational Behavior*, Barry M. Staw, ed., Glenview, IL: Scott, Foresman, 1982, pp. 161-168). The researchers attempted to persuade MBA students that a particular company was committed to avoiding layoffs. Four different techniques were used, one with each of four groups: telling a story, using statistics, using the story plus statistics, and sharing a policy statement issued by the company. The students who were given only the anecdote believed the company's claims more than students in any of the other groups did.

Naturally, anecdotes won't work best in every situation. *Nothing* works best in every situation. But you will often find this particular tool effective in gaining acceptance for you and your proposal.

Use Anecdotes as Antidotes

Smart Managing Pick up a copy of David M. Armstrong's *Managing by Storying Around: A New Method of Leadership* (New York: Doubleday, 1992). Learn how stories are being used as a powerful management tool.

Self-Deprecate. From time to time, we all face embarrassing or awkward situations at work. Those who self-deprecate usually find a gracious way out of the difficulty. In the process, they often win over those who had been dubious or opposed. You'll find your own words for doing this, but the real-life example of Orson Welles, who once had to lecture to a *very* small audience, illustrates the value of humor.

"I'm a director of plays," he informed them, "a producer of plays. I'm an actor of the stage and motion pictures. I'm a writer and producer of motion pictures. I write, direct, and act on the radio. I'm a magician and a painter. I've published books. I play the violin and the piano."

He paused then in the recitation of his accomplishments. He looked out at his audience and asked with genuine sadness in his voice, "Isn't it a pity there's so many of me and so few of you?"

Appeal to Common Sense. Nearly everyone is swayed by logical arguments. If you can defuse emotional volatility, then you can appeal to the common sense on which your ideas are based. When people are listening with open minds, when they've put aside personality problems or political issues, your leadership project can get the attention it deserves. Remember, though, starting with logic may not work. You may have to sweep away the irrelevant issues before you can get others to listen with disinterest to your idea.

Reference Current Events. Politicians use recent events all of the time to validate their calls to action. You can do the same. If, for example, you feel strongly about the need for training on financial matters and if you're lucky enough to have found a recent article substantiating the savings derived from such training, then your persuasion work is done for you. The more you can validate the need for your proposals with recent statistics, the more likely you are to persuade.

Point out the WIIFM Factor. Wanting to know how you'll benefit from a given proposal is natural. It doesn't mean you're selfish or unethical or unconcerned about others. Asking, "What's in it for me?" (WIIFM) is a normal reaction to a new idea. The wise leader knows this and works to provide the WIIFM Factor before it's even needed.

Use Appropriate Humor. You can often prevent an attack from becoming vicious by using humor that makes a point without being too pointed. A good source to cite is Dolly Parton. "I'm never offended by dumb blonde jokes," she once revealed. "That's because I know I'm not dumb. ... I also know I'm not blonde." You could use her quotation and then paraphrase it: "Joe, I'm not offended by your calling this proposal stupid, because I know it's not stupid. I just need a little more time to convince you of how smart it really is."

Liberate

To help inventiveness escape from the layers of "don'ts" and "can'ts" and "shouldn'ts" that have buried it, you have to scrape away old patterns of thinking. "A foolish consistency," after all, "is the hobgoblin of little minds."

When you liberate thinking, you offer others insights and innovation that could not have been gleaned from typical and traditional views. As a leader, you have an obligation to do this.

"How?" you may be wondering. Here's how.

Think Janusian Thoughts. You can inspire free thinking by asking others to imitate Janus, the Roman god whose profile is found on ancient coins. When you think in Janusian terms, you are bringing in an opposite point of view. Such thinking led to clever results like these:

- The popular television series *Columbo* permitted the audience to meet the murderer within the first few minutes of the story. Typically, in murder mysteries, the audience doesn't learn who the murderer is until the very end of the story.
- Retail merchants know the value of using opposites. "Christmas in July" is a popular theme for sales.
- Charles Kuralt explained the success of interviewing author Studs Terkel in Janusian terms. "When Studs Turkel listens," Kuralt observed, "everybody talks."
- Traditional management had managers doing performance ratings on their subordinates. Today, with 360° evaluations, subordinates are given the opportunity to evaluate the performance of their managers.

Think Outlandish Thoughts. From time to time, ask yourself and your team questions such as these:

- If money were no object, what would we do to solve this problem?
- If we were starting all over again, how would we handle this problem?
- If we didn't have to get anyone's approval, how would we proceed?

The provocative, even absurd question often serves as floss to remove the plaque with which time encrusts our ways of thinking.

Think Kinesthetic Thoughts. Liberate your thinking by thinking in a truly atypical way: use kinesthesia. This word refers to the mixing of senses and the expression of one in terms usually reserved for another. For example, if you could taste hatred,

---

Einstein Can't Be Wrong

It was Albert Einstein's contention that imagination is more important than knowledge. His thoughts are echoed by a more contemporary voice—Tom Peters—insisting that "imagination is the only source of real value in the new economy." Knowledge, in a sense, *is* power. However, if that statement were absolutely true, then librarians would rule the world. And we all know they don't.

Because so many people have access to the same knowledge—given all the books we can access in libraries free of charge and all the Web sites we can visit almost free of charge—imagination or the smart use of knowledge is what differentiates winners and losers.

---

would it taste like vinegar or cotton candy? The pragmatists among you are probably saying, "But you can't taste hatred."

For just a moment, assume that you can. Extend this kind of thinking to various problems or workplace scenarios. At the very least, you'll stumble upon some novel definitions. As an illustration, consider the anonymous observer who described architecture as "frozen music."

Resuscitate

The old, the discarded, the unused, the no-longer-popular can be a source of new ideas. Or, as the once-popular song goes, "Everything old is new again." Try resuscitating some practices, processes, procedures, philosophies, and abandoned plans from the past. Ordinarily, they represent considerable effort that's been expended. Parts of that effort may still be salvaged for contemporary purposes.

To facilitate your thinking along these lines, ask veteran employees, "What exactly made the good old days so good?"

Convergent Skills

There's a time and place for everything, including convergent thinking. Such thinking, in terms of problem-solving, parallels the scientific method. This method begins with a careful and precise definition of the problem. Next comes the generation of possible solutions, followed by the selection of the most promising of those solutions. That solution is then implemented and data are gathered to measure the effectiveness of the solution.

A variation on this method is the Plan-Do-Check-Act (PDCA) method popularized by Dr. W. Edwards Deming. The cycle begins again if the data indicate that calibration is needed in the original plan.

The following four-step plan—Pact, Act, Fact, Tact—encourages convergent thought, as do the Scientific Method and the PDCA Cycle. However, it incorporates the special skills leaders need as they solve problems with followers.

Pact

Leaders don't work in isolation. They establish connections with their immediate followers but also network with others at various levels inside and outside the organization. It's a waste of everyone's time, though, to make those connections without having a plan of attack. The "Pact" aspect of this plan asks you to get buy-in for your idea long before launching it.

You can develop the commitment you'll need by having answers ready for the tough questions team members typically have:

- How does this plan differ from what we already have?
- Why should we embrace this change?
- Where will we find the time to participate?
- What do we need to know before we join in?
- What proof do you have that this isn't just another flash in the pan?
- How much support is there for this at the upper levels?
- What's in it for me?
- Who benefits and how from this?
- What's the budget allocation?

Don't expect others to involve themselves, don't think commitment will simply happen unless and until you can answer these and other questions. By thoroughly exploring the pros and cons of your plan, you can determine who's willing to become a

---

What Lights Your Fire?

When you meet with your pact-partners, take a few moments to learn what *they're* all about. Ask each person to write down the answer to this question: "As far as work is concerned, what lights your fire?"

After a few minutes, ask them the second question: "As far as work is concerned, what burns you up?" (Note: if you simply ask them to speak out, to think on the spot, everyone will wind up repeating what the first person said. By asking them to write down their individual answers first, you'll get original and meaningful answers.)

With these two questions, you'll learn very quickly what idiosyncrasies might weaken the pact.

---

pact-partner and who would be a fair-weather soldier in the struggles that are sure to come.

Act

Once you have the commitment of your team, you can begin to act on the plan. This means answering the familiar five W's and an H.

- *Why* is this change better than what we've known?
- *Who* will be impacted/involved?
- *What* exactly does the change involve?
- *Where* will we begin? *Where* will we end?
- *When* is each stage scheduled for completion?
- *How* will the plan be executed?

Essentially, action involves deciding what has to be done, by whom, by when.

Fact

"What gets measured, gets done." A corollary to this well-known business axiom is this: "What gets measured may not get done." In other words, if the fact-finding stage of your plan reveals the plan is not working as well as you'd hoped, you may have to abandon it. Or, at the very least, make some adjustments.

Leaders don't fear negative feedback. In fact, they welcome it. Their egos are secondary issues because the primary issue is

> **⚠ CAUTION!**
> ### Make Room for Morphs
> Just as your solution to the problem may undergo radical change as the facts come in, so too may the problem itself change. Remain open to the possibility that the issue you identified is not the real problem.

the success of the plan. Leaders would rather know than not know the extent to which their ideas really are improvements over the old way of doing things.

There are many ways to gather the data you'll need to make your decisions. You can tabulate results from pre- and post-intervention surveys. You can gather anecdotal information. You can keep records and charts and tables. You can measure time and cost and the number of steps. The data you choose to record will depend, of course, on the nature of the plan you're implementing. Just make sure to keep everyone informed who needs to be. And if the results are disappointing, report those as honestly as you would report the good news.

Tact

No matter what conclusion the facts lead you to, you will need tact in relaying those results. If the measurements indicate success, you don't want to gloat when you report them to the initial doubters. Nor do you want to appear vain to early supporters. Instead, find a way to thank both groups.

The first group probably helped you strengthen your position (although you may not have realized it at the time). Their skepticism probably made you more determined to avoid potential pitfalls.

You can thank the second group by remaining committed to the project and by extending its success to other people, other places.

Use both tact and discretion in sharing results with various stakeholders. Not everyone needs to know everything. Decide with team members who needs what parts of the project's written history.

The leader in you has other decisions to make as well:

- Do you want to continue working as a team?
- If not, do you want to replace the whole team or just certain members?
- What can you say to team members who no longer wish to be part of the project?
- What if other divisions request help in implementing your idea at their locations?
- How can you best thank the team for the effort they have expended?

In thinking through the answers to questions like these, you'll need tact and diplomacy. To reject people and possibilities calls for outstanding leadership language.

Types of Thinking, Revisited

The popular terms for divergent and convergent skills are "right-brain" and "left-brain" thinking. Whatever you call the approaches, you'll have to admit they are different.

Divergent problem-solving relies on intuition, on the macrocosmic view, on the creative and spontaneous. Divergent thinkers see what everyone else is *not* seeing. They're subjective, as opposed to objective, in their rule-bending and rule-breaking. They *deviate*—by juxtaposing disparate elements, by taking on different roles, by personifying problems.

They also know ideas have to *incubate*, and so they listen patiently to inner voices and outside influence. Some ideas can't be rushed and the leader as problem-solver knows the importance of gestation. Before letting ideas die a premature death in the womb of disapproval, leaders win over converts. They often, for example, ask for a trial period for evaluating the project's success.

When leaders *obviate*, they defy the naysayers. They challenge themselves and others to higher levels of accomplishment. They do this, in part, by employing various persuasion techniques: citing precedents, current events, statistics, and higher authorities; turning criticism into questions; using anecdotes, humor, and self-deprecating remarks; appealing to common sense; and pointing out the WIIFM elements.

Liberate is another important verb in the leader's vocabulary. In liberating herself and others from the prison of hackneyed and overused concepts, the leader may think in Janusian terms. She may also think outlandishly, taking to heart Tom Peters' assertion that "every organization needs at least one weirdo on staff." Kinesthetic thinking, which mixes and matches the senses, is another means of freeing creativity.

Finally, divergent thinkers often turn to the past. They *resuscitate* old ideas, even some from different arenas, and make them applicable to the present.

Convergent thinkers, by contrast, depend on logic and the comfortable reassurances derived from the scientific approach. They think critically, attend to details, and rely on metrics for determining the best steps in the problem-solving process.

They create a *pact* with their followers, gaining consensus before making assignments. Then they *act*, ensuring the carefully prepared plan has an executor and a timetable for each part of the plan. The *fact* is preferred to the fantasy of thinking all is going well. Leaders who converge on a given outcome do so because quantifiable data tell them they should. Finally, these leaders use *tact* to share results, both good and bad.

Manager's Checklist for Chapter 3

❑ Create a climate of creativity in your organization.

❑ Use both convergent and divergent thinking.

❑ Realize not all problems require the same approach. Try more than one approach to problem-solving if the first isn't working.

❑ Don't be a victim of your culture. Look beyond the familiar.

❑ Extend your range of requisite behaviors.

❑ Don't try to hurry to reach decisions. Take the time necessary to think things through.

❏ Review and prioritize problems with your staff every three months.

❏ Recognize that knowledge and imagination are both important for leaders.

❏ Apply the Plan-Do-Check-Act (also known as the Shewhart Cycle) system of solving problems.

❏ Know your staff. Ask what lights their fires and what burns them up.

The Leader as Team-Builder

Don Petersen, former head of Ford Motor Company, maintained that results depend on relationships. It's nearly impossible to lead if you can't develop cooperative working relationships. Leaders who can't build teams don't deserve the title.

Team-building is the process of developing a cohesive group of individuals committed to working cooperatively. Typically, the members of such teams are high-performing individuals, eager to pursue organizational aims.

The Big Picture

Given the stress associated with work today and the further stress related to working closely with others, we can easily fall into the trap of focusing too narrowly on microcosmic concerns and neglecting the macrocosmic mission. The leader as team-builder must ensure all team members understand the big picture and put it above petty personal issues.

Such a leader also recognizes "we" as the operative word in groups assembled not to find fault, but to find better ways of con-

verting inputs to quality outputs. As part of her big-picture thinking, the leader who builds teams knows the behavior that gets
rewarded gets repeated. She knows the rapidity with which team
commitment dies is inversely proportional to the speed and intensity of upper management response to the team's efforts.

Consequently, this leader views herself as a critical link
between the team she leads and the managers she reports to.

Leaders and managers
alike need a sense of the
big picture, and they need
to maintain all the details
that constitute that big picture. In metaphoric terms,
they need both the "bird's
eye" view of the situation
and the "worm's eye" view.
There is a simple test to
see if you view situations
from both angles.

It consists of a single
question—and the answer
to this question is not as
important as the way the
answer comes into your
mind. The framework for

> ### A Team by Any Other Name
>
> The quality movement has spawned a number of terms for teams: process action team, process improvement team, cross-functional team, self-directed work team, ad hoc team, etc. No matter what they're called, no matter how permanent they are, no matter how critical their function, high-performing teams share certain characteristics. They are composed of six to eight members, they meet regularly, they are diverse in make-up, they have a strong leader and a clear mission, and they have a "champion" who serves as their advocate.

the answer is your life between the ages of five and 10 (or the
years between kindergarten and fifth grade). Again, try to focus
on *how* the answer comes to you, rather than the answer itself.
Ready? Here's the question. During the first few years when you
were in school, who was your favorite teacher?

How did that answer come to you? Did you see his or her
face? Did you remember his or her name? Or did you see and
hear the face and name at the same time? If both face and
name came to you, you probably have the enviable skill of
being able to look at things through both a wide-angle and a
zoom lens.

Mission

Keeping the mission uppermost in your mind will help you fashion outcomes that come close to your intentions. One way to do this is to begin every exchange—no matter with whom, no matter what the problem or why the team has convened—with a statement of purpose. Think back to the least successful interpersonal exchange of which you have ever been part. What statement could have been made at the beginning of that exchange (and referred to subsequently) to help ensure positive results?

To shape successful outcomes for exchanges with team members, think of at least five mission-relevant openings that set a positive tone for the meeting. One might be "We're on this team because we both believe in what we're doing. Let's keep our mission in mind as we meet today." Once you've compiled your list, commit to using one new opening each month.

Ground Rules

Ground rules help shape meetings that are productive expenditures of time. Make a list of 10 that ideally will govern future interactions. If such rules already exist for your team, reduce your existing list to a single one. Or, develop your team's own paraphrase of this Henry Ford observation: "Coming together is a beginning; keeping together is progress; and working together is success."

Post your rules and/or your Ford paraphrase so it's clearly visible whenever you meet.

Personalities

Hatim Tyabji, CEO of Verifone, once observed that success at work today is composed of 5% technical knowledge and 95% psychology. The composite picture of your team is actually a mosaic—uncountable personality traits and quirks that ultimately combine for success or failure. The more you understand what drives behavior, the better you can work with others.

How would you describe your own personality? Under what conditions do you do your very best work? When are you difficult

---

Open-Ended Beginnings

To achieve unanimity of thought regarding purpose, ask each
team member, early in the life of the team, to complete these
statements on paper.

* This team exists to ...
* We value ...
* Our desired outcome(s) is/are ...
* We can measure our effectiveness when we ...

Then compare your reply with the replies given by the others on
your team. Discuss the discrepancies and formulate a statement of purpose that can be used for later progress reports to senior management.

---

to work with? What compromises would you be willing to make
to achieve the end result? Does your team know the answer to
these questions? Do you know their answers to the same questions? Spend some time discussing the issues these questions
evoke.

How Flexible Are You?

If we regard leadership on a continuum—with the autocratic
leader at one end, the *laissez-faire* leader at the other, and the
democratic or participative leader in the middle—where would
you place yourself? Place an "X" on the following continuum to
show your leadership style.

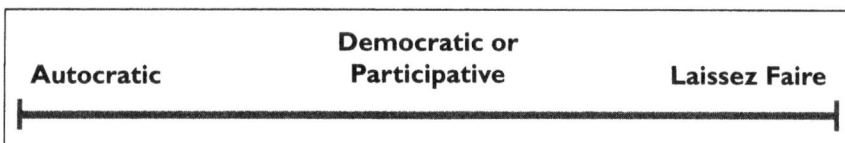

	Democratic or	
Autocratic	**Participative**	**Laissez Faire**
├──┤		

Figure 4-1. Leadership style continuum

If you subscribe to Fred Fiedler's Contingency Theory, you
wouldn't have been able to place an "X" anywhere. Why?
Because Fiedler says your style should vary. It should move
along the continuum, depending on the nature of the task, the
nature of the people who perform the task, and the conditions
under which they have to perform it.

Flexibility comes in many forms. There's emotional flexibility, verbal flexibility, physical flexibility, mental flexibility, and so

on. If you have psychological flexibility, for example, you can quickly assess a situation, make adjustments to your intended actions, and succeed in having the exchange turn out with wins for all concerned.

Flexibility comes into play for team leaders as well. If you think about it, you're not the same person every day. You perform various roles on various days. Think about some of the roles you performed this week. Did you serve as a minister, a traffic cop, an orchestra leader? Were you called upon to be a coach, a judge, a detective?

No doubt you played many roles. And your team members will have to play differing roles, too, in order for the team as a whole to succeed.

While successful teams have members playing various roles, those roles fall into two broad categories. *Task* roles relate to mission accomplishment. *Maintenance* roles relate to harmonious interactions among team members.

Think about videotaping a team meeting so you can analyze the contributions of various people. Doing so will not only help your present team function more efficiently, but also help individual members perform better in the future as they serve on other teams.

> **TRICKS OF THE TRADE**
>
> ### Circle-Locution
>
> A simple method of analyzing team interactions calls for one person (perhaps even an outside observer) to draw a circle representing the table at which the team sits. He then writes the names of team members according to where they sit around the table. During the course of the meeting, this person draws an arrow each time one person speaks to another and a wavy line each time someone addresses the team as a whole.
>
> Analyzing this simple diagram after the meeting will yield you insights into participants' levels of contribution.

Who Performs the Task Roles?

Understanding the various task behaviors will give you a sense of the big picture of contributions. Some specific task behaviors and examples of them follow.

Initiating	Suggests courses of action
Seeking information	Asks questions
Giving information	Volunteers examples
Clarifying	Asks for explanations, repetition
Summarizing	Periodically provides overview of what's been discussed
Building consensus	Knows and uses tools for reaching (near) agreement
Emphasizing purpose	Keeps meeting within framework of mission
Monitoring time	Tells team when discussion are straying or taking too long
Offering alternatives	Moves stalled action forward by suggesting other options

Who Performs the Maintenance Roles?

Effective team members intensify the drama of team meetings by playing various roles. When they work to build relationships, they are performing maintenance tasks. Some of these important tasks are described as follows.

Harmonizing	Provides the "social glue" that keeps members connected
Encouraging	Moves people from discouragement to possibility
Compromising	Helps achieve buy-in for a workable solution
Admonishing	Gently rebukes when necessary
Praising	Offers sincere recognition of effort
Inviting contributions	Ensures all members are heard from
Intervening	Helps disputing members work cooperatively
Identifying blocks	Reminds team of areas of agreement, identifies barriers

Letter Man or Woman

You've probably heard the popular definition of "team": Together, Each Achieves More.

The next time your team convenes, toss out a short, work-related word and ask for a comparable acronymic definition.

Here's an alternative. Select a given letter, such as "C." Have each team member contribute a word that begins with the same letter and relates to the mission.

Expectations for Team Members

In addition to the task and maintenance roles you expect your team to play, you need to make clear the other behaviors you expect. (It's so much easier to lead when people understand and agree to a common set of rules.)

Tell your staff or team that being on a team means meeting certain requirements:

- Know the mission.
- Share glory with others.
- Contribute.
- Respect others.
- Have requisite knowledge.
- Let the leader lead.
- Show willingness to sacrifice on occasion.
- Compromise.
- Try something new.
- Do your homework.
- Speak up if something is bothering you.
- Keep an open mind.
- Try to understand other people's viewpoint.
- Listen.
- Offer alternatives.
- Know that you make a difference.

Differing Skills

Leadership demands many things of you. Among your most important responsibilities is that of aligning tasks with talent. It's not as simple as it may initially seem. Complicating the alignment is the fact that some people may be good at some things but would prefer not to do them. And some people who don't yet have a particular talent may be interested in acquiring it. To be sure, deadline pressure means that time dominates all other considerations. Finishing a project is more important than training unskilled members. And yet, the experience of working on the project provides the best training some currently unskilled members will ever have.

Too, you have to balance personalities. A brilliant but cantankerous team member should perhaps be asked to work on his assignment in isolation. To team him with a new or less-skilled person may cause irreparable divisions in the team.

Orchestrating all these factors is the reason teams need leaders. As you carry out this complex and sometimes subjective job, keep in mind the word "diverse." Ideally, your team will be composed of at least one person who is creative, at least one person who is logical, and at least one person who is knowledgeable about the process.

You can help smooth out the edges created by differences in skill levels by asking members to evaluate the team's progress and their personal contribution. Devise a simple questionnaire that members can submit anonymously if they choose to do so. Periodically invite feedback with questions such as the following:

- "How can I help you?"
- "What would you like to see done differently?"
- "What would make us more cohesive?"
- "What would you like to know more about?"

A true team succeeds or fails as an entire unit. And the leader is judged by the success or failure of his or her team. The success of one particular team member is a shared success, not an individual glory. The leader is an integral part of the team. When it succeeds, he succeeds. When it fails, he fails, too.

To help ensure the former scenario, the leader works to build a team with extensive expertise. The greater the depth of the team's experience, the greater the overall contribution it can make to the mission. The leader pulls forth the best from each member, seeking to supplement possible weaknesses by adding a new member or arranging for additional training as required.

Rewards

Research from Fred Herzberg and many others repeatedly shows that money is not the primary reward for working adults. In your leadership role, you can provide rewards that cost little but produce much in terms of satisfaction. Take the time to work on the following exercise. You'll see what we mean. (You may wish to make several copies of the exercise before marking on it.)

From the following list, prioritize (1 = your top choice) the top six items that would make you feel most rewarded for having done a good job.

___ a. gift certificate
___ b. time off (in terms of hours, not days)
___ c. a letter of recognition
___ d. a ceremony to which your family members are invited
___ e. the opportunity to serve on another team
___ f. an invitation to share your success with other teams
___ g. a newspaper article about your team's efforts
___ h. cash award
___ i. a celebration, such as a picnic
___ j. one-month membership in a health club
___ k. having the division head made aware of the team's effort
___ l. a hobby-related gift
___ m. a call from the head of the organization
___ n. your choice of a parking spot
___ o. having the whole team taken out to dinner
___ p. more training opportunities
___ q. tickets to a concert
___ r. being asked for your opinion on subsequent projects

Now, get inside the head of each member of your team. Do

a separate list for each person on your team, identifying the top six priorities you think that person would list. Then, give each person a blank copy of the list and ask him or her to select their own priorities. Compare those answers with what you assumed they would value. If there is a match in most cases, you should commend yourself for truly knowing your team.

On the other hand, if there are some surprises, you profit in two ways. One, you find some inexpensive ways to recognize and reward. Two, you learn once again the danger of making assumptions.

> **Tuckman's Trick**
>
> Bruce Tuckman, more than 30 years ago, composed a four-word rhyme to delineate the stages of team formation: Form, Storm, Norm, Perform. Write a similar four-word rhyme to depict the process of rewarding team members.

Teamwork Is Its Own Reward

When teamwork works, it becomes its own reward. In view of this assertion, rate the extent to which your current team reflects these optimal conditions. Use "A" for "Definitely describes us," "B" for "This is true to some extent," and "C" for "This is not true of us."

___ a. The mission toward which we're working is challenging.

___ b. The tasks can be completed in the amount of time we have been given.

___ c. Our work conditions allow us to concentrate.

___ d. The goals have been clearly defined.

___ e. We are able to obtain feedback on our progress easily.

___ f. We have an appropriate degree of both authority and responsibility.

___ g. Our individual concerns recede as the team's accomplishments take on greater and greater significance.

___ h. We have become more self-confident since we first formed this team.

___ i. We feel justifiable pride in our accomplishments.

You'll glean a deeper understanding of how well your team functions as a unit if you ask the members to do the same assessment. Uncover discrepancies. Discover new ways to enhance your productivity.

Conflicts

In a sense, when team members feel passionate enough about a position to argue for it, they are demonstrating their commitment to success. On the other hand, such passion can lead to flareups. In the following sections, we'll deal with techniques for resolving the conflicts born of dedication to the best possible outcome, as well as those born of less honorable reasons.

An anonymous sage once observed that every great oak was once a nut that stood its ground. Unfortunately, if everyone stands her own ground, the separate trees, metaphorically speaking, will never make a forest. Think of a serious argument that's erupted between two members of your team (past or present), each of whom clung fiercely to her own point of view. What techniques have you used successfully in the past to work out a compromise in cases like this? What techniques have you seen or heard others use successfully?

If conflict is dividing your team, commit to finding one additional technique before the month ends. You can turn to the Internet, books, magazine articles, or even other managers.

> ### Don't Tell Me to Calm Down!
>
> **Smart Managing** Psychologists tell us that asking an angry person to "calm down" is likely to have just the opposite effect. What two sentences should others *not* say to you when you are in a "flareup" mode? What two sentences *would* help extinguish your personal anger flames?
>
> Over time, ask each member of your team the same two questions and keep a list of the replies you receive.

Among the elements shared by high-performing teams are:

- Refusal to waste time
- Spirit of creativity

- Willingness to probe beneath the surface
- Debate that doesn't offend but examines every facet of the issue
- Emphasis on not making the same mistake twice, rather than on pointing fingers
- Recognition of the importance of keeping appropriate others informed.

Optimizing these six elements can lead to great achievement. Minimized, they can be the source of great conflict. In which of these elements is your team strongest? Weakest?

The Delphi Oracle asserted you should know yourself. As a leader, you should know your team. Give further thought to the last two questions you answered. Then list three ways to assess or improve the answers you gave.

Consensus

The Delphi Technique. You can stand up for what you believe without standing apart from the team or the team purpose. Achieving respect for all ideas is often a matter of knowing the tools for doing so.

The Delphi Technique has been used for thousands of years when teams reach a roadblock on the road to consensus. Here's how it works. When the topics are controversial, delicate, and/or emotion-laden, the team leader calls a halt to the proceedings and asks members to honestly and anonymously submit a short statement of their feelings about the subject and their recommendations for resolution.

If necessary, a facilitator can be brought in to help the team find a middle ground that synthesizes both extremes.

Consensus-Builders. Here are several statements that will help you express your point of view when others may be trying to control you, the exchange, and perhaps even the outcome.

a. "I listened without interruption as you made your point. Now, please extend the same courtesy to me."
b. "What could I say or do that would bring closure here? (or

What could I say or do that would satisfy you?) Now...
here's what *I* feel would bring closure."

c. "That is not germane to the issue." (Repeat several
times.)

d. "I can see how strongly you feel about this. I need some
time, too, to separate the emotion from the issue. Let me
get back to you."

e. "I prefer not to discuss this now." (Then, walk away.)

f. "It's important for us to remember the whole is greater
than the sum of its parts. I think we both need to give a
little with our respective parts so we create that 'whole.'"

g. "I don't think either one of us is really hearing the other.
Why don't we take a 10-minute break to write down our
points of view and then exchange them with each other?"

h. "Hold on a minute. I don't think that's a fair statement."

i. "I can feel my blood pressure rising. Let me see if I can
get it back down again by restating the facts here without
emotional associations."

What others can you add to this list? If you prefer, create a
separate list for a third-person, neutral party to use when two
team members are conflicting.

Meetings

In all sizes, shapes, and spaces (including the cyber one), people form teams and meet to achieve goals. When you lead your
team in meetings, you should always have an agenda, with time
allocations beside the various items. Ideally, you can distribute
the agenda several days before the meeting so participants can
come prepared.

At the very beginning of the meeting, appoint a time monitor, someone who will ensure that the group adheres to the time
allocations, and a topic monitor, who will get the group back on
track, if necessary. There should also be a scribe, so you can
focus more on group dynamics and less on the recording
requirements. (Unrelated but valuable digressions can be listed
on "Parking Lot" chart paper.)

Our Debt to C. Crawford

TRICKS OF THE TRADE

Were you thinking "C" stood for Cindy? Actually, the Crawford we meant is C.C. Crawford, a professor at the University of Southern California. His technique helps teams achieve consensus through the sheer force of numbers.

First, write the problem so everyone can see it. Then, give each person 10 small sheets of paper. Within 10 minutes, they have to record 10 separate solutions for the problem, one per sheet of paper. (Note: People will complain, after the first five minutes, that they can't think of anything else. Encourage them to keep thinking: the best ideas usually come near the end of the session, after all the obvious answers have been written down.)

A volunteer then collects the papers, leaves the room to sort them all out, and returns to make a report. The volunteer tells which choices were the most popular and also which were the most viable or most inventive. The team then votes on the top five choices the volunteer has recommended.

Teams composed of individuals vying for power and visibility can make meeting rooms miniature torture chambers. It's the team leader's job to help members function as an integrated whole. If others follow your lead, you'll see behavior so smooth that the overall objective takes precedence over individual priorities. In the ideal team, members let go of their ego drive and seek instead the synergy that is released when people are committed to collaborative interaction.

Autocratic behavior on the part of the team leader simply does not work, except in crisis situations. Employees today are more independent than ever. They seek fulfillment and satisfaction in their jobs and the kind of pride associated with team accomplishment. They are willing to give but they expect to get. And when teams function well, when skills are blended and conflict is resolved, members *do* get a return on their effort investment. They get back the satisfaction that can come only from accomplishment.

Keys to Successful Teams

Successful teams do not happen overnight. They are the result of a long-term commitment from both management and team members. This commitment is a commitment to training and growth. It is also a commitment to relinquish individualistic concerns for the greater good of the team.

Keep the big picture in mind whenever your team assembles. It will help put the minor squabbles and stressors in their rightful place—beneath the overarching mission. But don't have so lofty a view that you overlook the "worm's eye" details that can sink your team.

Frequent references to mission and strict adherence to ground rules will help your team meet its primary objective. Of course, different personalities and differing skill levels can present occasional barriers. Remain as flexible as you can when disruptions arise. And, be sure to employ both task and maintenance skills as you keep the team on track and happy to be there.

Conflict, if channeled properly, can actually strengthen your team. But you have to know the tools for channeling, such as the Delphi Technique, the Crawford Technique, and consensus-building statements.

Consensus means achievement. And achievement means rewarding your team. The rewards you present them need not cost anything at all. But they should be rewards in the team's eyes, not only yours. Ask members how they'd like to be recognized and then apply your creativity to novel expressions of appreciation.

Finally, pledge to more efficient meetings by having an agenda, a time monitor, a topics monitor, and a scribe whenever your team convenes.

Manager's Checklist for Chapter 4

❏ Work hard to obtain upper management's support for your team's work.

❏ Find a "champion" to support your team.

❑ Begin meetings and interpersonal exchanges with a statement of purpose.

❑ Work together to create ground rules. Post them. Refer to them.

❑ Ask people to complete statements. Then discuss discrepancies.

❑ Read books or articles on human psychology in order to understand your followers better.

❑ Remain flexible. Know that your style should vary according to the task, the conditions, and the people working on the task.

❑ Learn more about your team by having an observer note the contributions of people at the meeting.

❑ Let your followers know your expectations.

❑ When appropriate, have new or unskilled members learn "on the job."

❑ Make everyone aware of the value of diversity.

❑ Get feedback on how the team functions by asking specific questions and letting members reply anonymously.

❑ Poll members to learn what they want in terms of rewards.

❑ Study the techniques that work to resolve conflict.

❑ Have prepared statements ready for tense situations.

❑ Put good ideas that you don't have time to discuss at team meetings in the "parking lot."

The Leader as Manager

Apart from your *official* duties as a leading manager, you manage ever so many other things. You "manage" to keep your eye on the ball, your nose to the grindstone, your ear to the ground, your finger on the pulse of the times, your mind on the task, your thoughts to yourself, your feet on the ground, your back to the wall, your shoulder to the wheel, and your head on straight. You manage time and tension, emotions and energy, schedules and stress, projects and priorities, data and deadlines.

If the last decade of the twentieth century represented the "nanosecond nineties," we can be sure that the first ten of the new century are not going to slow down a bit, and the pace of change will probably increase. More than ever before, you will need new ways to manage and, in so doing, gain control of events that often seem to be spiraling toward chaos. If you can manage yourself, stress, time, energy, and emotions well, you will surely manage others better. You can even take the lead in helping them manage themselves better as well.

Melt the Snow of Many Winters

As you learning more about managing work-related and life-related elements, keep in mind the story of the little boy who was found sobbing in the cloak room by his first grade teacher. She promptly bent down to comfort him. "What's wrong, Sammy?" she asked gently.

He told her that his boots were missing.

"No, Sammy," she gently corrected him. "These are your boots, right here." They were the only pair left. She knew they had to be his.

His tears did not subside, however. "Those aren't mine," he insisted amid hiccoughs. "Mine had snow on them!"

Over the course of your management career, you've probably allowed the "snow" of long-standing habits to harden your perspective. There's nothing wrong with that. That hardening represents your survivability. Nonetheless, you have to let some new ideas penetrate that frozen crust from time to time. You have to let some snow melt so you can adopt some new survival strategies.

Managing Stress

As a manager, you've probably allowed habits to harden your perspective, to help you survive. But you have to let some new ideas penetrate; you have to adopt some new survival strategies.

Some of those strategies may relate to stress. Stress is the natural and normal reaction to events that occur regularly and less frequently. When you fail to control stress or cope with it, you may experience *dis*tress. When you handle it well, when you use stress to give you the drive you need to compete and to succeed, then you experience *eu*stress. There is the "good stress," for example, that a bride experiences on her wedding day and the "bad stress" that we experience when things get out of control.

A related problem is burnout, which is usually associated with work. If your job is causing an ongoing deterioration in your ability to cope, if it's causing mental, physical, and emotional exhaustion, then you may be experiencing burnout. You can recharge your batteries and restore optimism, but if you're unwilling or unable to rejuvenate, then the cumulative effect can be very damaging indeed.

Management is typically a highly stressful profession, one in which burnout occurs frequently. One way to judge if you're a candidate for burnout is to ask yourself the following questions:

- Are my expectations too high?
- Am I constantly seeking perfection?
- Do I have trouble admitting problems?
- Have others mentioned the possibility of burnout to me?
- Am I expecting more of my staff than they can give?

Stress takes its toll on us in various ways. And when the stress is prolonged or too intense, it ultimately has a serious effect on both the mind and the body. A secondary difficulty with stress is the ripple effects. When you succumb to it, you affect others in uncountable negative ways.

What symptoms do you experience when you're stressed?

Review these common reactions to stress. Check those you've experienced in the last two years. Circle those you've experienced in the last six months.

___ Blurred vision	___ Migraines
___ Nervous breakdown	___ Cancer
___ Rash, hives, allergies, asthma	___ Unusual sweating
___ Sudden, unexplainable fear	___ Violence
___ Personality changes	___ Unusual fatigue
___ Negative thinking, talking	___ Headaches
___ Shivering	___ Mood swings
___ Sleeping too much	___ Anger
___ Rheumatoid arthritis	___ Stroke
___ Hypertension	___ Ulcers
___ Nervous laughter	___ Temper tantrums
___ Numbness	___ Sleeplessness
___ Irritability	___ Excessive eating
___ Frequent illness	___ Twitches

Lighten Up!

According to a survey by William M. Mercer, Inc. (reported in *Entrepreneur,* March 2000), only 8% of employers try to lighten the mood at work with fun activities.

Don't be part of that minority. Once a week, do something different and lighthearted for your staff. It can be as simple as a five-minute popcorn break or a competition to name the company baseball team. Given the tremendous costs associated with stress, you owe it to your team and your organization to lead team members away from tension and into good times.

Smart Managing

___ Increased drinking or smoking

___ Stuttering

___ Inability to concentrate

___ Hyperactivity

___ Muscle tension

___ Loss of appetite

___ Nervousness

___ Compulsive behavior

___ Teeth grinding

___ Hearing loss

___ Crying at inappropriate times

___ Anxiety

___ Withdrawal

___ Digestive problems

___ Dry mouth

___ Muscle spasms

___ Heart palpitations

___ Hair loss (temporary)

___ Sudden poor performance

___ Incessant talking

What Causes Stress?

Basically, when things—finances, career, relationships, health, etc.—are going the way we want them to go, we experience little or no stress. But when things are not turning out as we want them to, when we feel we are losing control of situations, then we begin to experience stress. Think about the "things" in your life. Which are turning out the way you expect them to? Which are not, despite your very best efforts?

Introspecting is one of the best ways to penetrate the crust we've been talking about. Answer this question: "How do you know when you've done a good job?" Not surprisingly, psychologists tell us that negative stress results when we feel we have little or no control over situations. One clue to your personal control factor may lie in the way you answered the good-job question. If you cited *others*—for example, "My boss tells me I've done a good job"—then the external-control quotient in your stress equation is probably pretty high. However, if you cited *yourself*—for example, "I am pleased with the results"— then your internal-control factor is probably quite healthy.

Think of all the things you do on a weekly basis. How many of them are you doing because of your own wishes and intents and how many are you doing because others expect or want you to? Express your answer as a percentage: to what extent do you feel "externally controlled"?

Another source of stress is change. Author Bruce Barton wisely comments, "When you're through changing, you're through." As fatalistic as the words sound, they do reinforce the fact that life is change. You'll go a long way toward diminishing the stress your followers experience if you can help them develop the right mindset toward change and if you can model acceptance.

You cannot change the changes, for life is a perpetually shifting mosaic. Permanence comes only when life has ended. But you *can* change your reactions to change. You can learn to view new situations as sources of challenge, not sources of distress. You can force yourself to consider innovation and altered circumstances as small miracles, offering us the opportunity for growth and an escape from boredom. Nothing remains forever. Given the inescapable fact that change is a normal part of life, you can develop the emotional resources to meet new challenges.

Try These Tips

1. Think globally. Act locally. Put the stress factor in perspective. Just think about what is happening in the world—earthquakes, floods, war, bombings, fires, terrorism. Then realize that the stressor you are facing is, in all likelihood, insignificant by comparison.

2. Change your thinking about criticism. View it as a possible

opportunity to learn more about yourself. And ...don't respond to it until you've put some distance between you and the critic or the critique.

3. De-stress yourself by becoming absorbed in someone else's life. You can read the biography of someone you admire (and feel de-stressed, probably, when you compare your problems with his). Or, you can get to know each of your team members better—one a week. Do this by asking a questions such as this: "Think about the various decades of your life. What incident from what decade comes to mind first?"

4. When you feel pressure building up, visualize your stress as a balloon about to pop. Then imagine letting out a little bit of air pressure over a two-minute span of time. This simple technique can help control tension when you feel you're ready to explode.

   On a related note, draw a simple "stressometer" in the shape of a thermometer every morning for the next three months. Indicate increments of 10 all the way to 100—just as a thermometer is marked to measure your temperature. Then, each day, as events unfold, gauge the amount of stress you are feeling and "accumulate" it graphically on the drawing. Ideally, you will not let your stress level rise too high on any given day.

   At the end of three months, review your stressometers to see if you have been exerting greater control over the stressors in your life.

5. Keep in mind what George Bernard Shaw had to say about our verbal connections: "The single biggest problem in communication is the illusion that it has taken place." Don't hesitate to repeat your message to ensure its clarity. (The average adult needs to hear about a new concept four times before the idea sinks in and becomes intellectual reality. For the average preschooler, it's 55 times!) When you rephrase your request, use different words and ask for feedback before moving along to a new idea.

Managing Time

Naturally, as a manager, you direct activities and control events so that goals are met within the appointed time frame. It's your professional obligation to do so. But your job is only part of your life. Ideally, you also have a personal obligation to use time well.

By this stage in your life, you have a fairly realistic sense of who you are and what you can do. But ... you're probably underestimating yourself. Chances are you're not taking advantage of the largeness and largess of the world. Scientists estimate that we're using only one-tenth of our brain capacity. (Einstein, by his own estimate, was using only one-quarter.) There is much more you can do, much more you can experience, much more you can attain. Let at least one of your management goals be a dream with deadlines.

Do not be like the child whose world-view was very limited. Asked how he could tell when a person was getting old, he replied, "They start to get ugly. This usually happens around age 30."

We can forgive this youthful distortion. But we cannot forgive the limiting views that we may be imposing on ourselves, such as thinking that 30 is old.

> **Smart Managing**
>
> ### Time for Goals
>
> Before you commit to improvements, try to establish an overarching view of time. It'll guide you through the tough decisions you have to make.
>
> In the macrocosmic sense, know what you wish to have or to have accomplished by your retirement. By age 25, 35, 45, or 55, if you're new to leadership. In the microcosmic sense, determine what you wish to accomplish each year, month, week, and day. You don't have to make elaborate plans or keep every detail in a day-planner. But you should know what your aspirations are before you can aspirate no more.

Ask Questions

To assist you in the management of time, formulate at least 10 questions and keep them near you as you make decisions about the best use of your time at any given moment. Here are a few to get you started.

1. Will this action bring me closer to my personal or professional goal?
2. Could I consider this a priority?
3. What would happen if I didn't do this or didn't do it right now?
4. Is there someone else who could do this for me?
5. How can I streamline this process?

Try These Tips

1. Forgive your mistakes ... and the mistakes of others. They weren't made intentionally, after all. Be guided by the words of Mother Teresa: "I feel like a pencil in God's hands.... God writes through us, and however imperfect instruments we may be, He writes beautifully." Keep your pencil tips sharpened, yes, so you can make the best use of time. But remind yourself periodically that pencils have erasers for a very good reason.

2. There are those who insist they can't prioritize because *everything* is a priority. If this statement is true for you, then it doesn't matter where you start. If the statement is not *really* true, then you can decide which is the number one priority and act accordingly. Priorities have to be viewed from a dual perspective:
   What is important in terms of long-range outcomes?
   What must be done immediately (regardless of its importance) because of its urgency?

3. A more formal method of deciding how to use time asks you to draw a simple matrix. Then assign valences or weights to each item according to both its importance and its urgency. Begin by making five columns on a sheet of paper. Label the first "Tasks" and five things you need to get done within the next week or so. Label the second column "Importance" and record the valence of each item: 1 = most important and 3 = least important. Next, label the third column "Urgency" and assign a weight here to each thing you have to do: 1= most urgent and 3 = least urgent. In the

It's All Relative

Smart Managing "Time is relative; its only worth depends upon what we do as it is passing." Einstein's words have relevance for leaders. When you lead, you have debts to fulfill. Followers have committed their time to you. As that time passes, you must maximize its value. Leaders who "wing it" usually wind up clipping the wings of time. Then, instead of soaring, the project usually falls to earth. If you don't have a plan, don't waste people's time.

fourth column, labeled "Weight," you will write the added score for each item. Finally, mark the fifth column "Priority" and prioritize. The lowest score becomes your top priority, etc.

4. To help you sort out which of your many management tasks deserve your immediate attention, ask yourself the four "T" questions:
   • Is the task due ... Today?
   • Is the task due ... Tomorrow?
   • Is the task ... Time-independent? (no actual deadline)
   • Is the task related to the ... True reason for your job's existence?

5. Divide each day by deadline dates: three hours for work due today, three hours for work due next week, one hour for work due next month, one-half hour for work due in six months, and leftover minutes for work due within the next year.

Managing Emotions

The possibility of violence in the workplace should disturb the emotional equilibrium of all managers. When you wear your *managerial* hat, you fulfill the requirements the organization has established. If there is no such set of guidelines to prevent workplace violence, for example, then you have to switch what's on your head and in your head.

You have to put on the *leadership* hat. When you wear this hat, you take a proactive role in convincing senior management of the need for training or programs or counseling. Such anger-management programs should be a priority—given the fact that 20 Americans die each week because of violence in the workplace.

Once you've worked to make the anti-violence policy known, then you can concentrate on managing emotions in a smaller realm. You can concentrate on controlling your own reactions and encouraging harmony among your staff.

"Emotional intelligence" is a term coined by Daniel Goleman (New York: Bantam Books, 1995). If you can lead your team to collectively exhibit such intelligence, you are pre-destining their success. In fact, Harvard University studied successful managers at the end of their careers. It asked them to retrospectively rate the relative importance of technical skills, job knowledge and attitude. The results: technical skills, 5%; job knowledge, 10%; and attitude, 85%.

To develop this kind of intelligence, get in the habit of using meta-cognition. In other words, as you're doing something, make yourself doubly aware of what you're doing. Rather than operate on a single plane of awareness, you can operate in a state of heightened awareness. During this attuned state, you may do some self-talking or see some "red flags."

Those who succumb to road rage, for example, operate in response to the trivialities of the moment. They're not taking the long-range view of potential consequences. They're not reminding themselves that *anger* is only one letter away from *danger*.

Leaders help others develop this emotional perspective. They push for attitudes of gratitude, for optimism in the face of seemingly insurmountable odds. They think like the child whose father took him fishing for the very first time. He waited impatiently as his father baited the lines and then cast them into the stream. The boy took the smaller rod from his father and, within moments, was certain he felt something wiggling at the end of his line. And he was right! With great glee, he reeled the line in and then proudly announced, "Look, Dad! I caught a worm!"

The choice is yours. You can appreciate the small victories as well as the large ones. Or you can be disgruntled, disagreeable, and disappointed over the fish you have not *yet* caught. Lead your staff to the kind of acceptance that has "try again" at its core.

Try These Tips

1. Have a "shelf-esteem," where you collect small symbols of accomplishments. Gaze at it whenever you feel discouraged. And let the sight of your children, or trophies, or commendations, or certificates melt the icicles of self-doubt that grow in all of our hearts from time to time. Establish such a shelf for your whole team, too.

2. Goleman reports on a study at Bell Labs in Naperville, Illinois. There, brilliant scientists pursue significant research projects. Some of those scientists, though, were derailed in their careers, never rising to the heights they and others had expected of them. The difference between the standout performers and the career-stalled employees boiled down to people skills. The high achievers had built people networks that served them in good stead when they needed help. The mediocre performers wasted time waiting for help to arrive from people with whom no relationships had been established. The lesson here: build a support system *before* you need to use it.

3. Do not permit the other person's negativity to infiltrate your own actions. While you can't control what others say or do, you *can* control your reactions. Smile pleasantly at curmudgeons and keep the words of someone like Morarji Desai, former Prime Minister of India, in mind: "Life at any time can become difficult. Life at any time can become easy. It all depends upon how one adjusts oneself to life."

4. Set a time limit for listening to complaints. Otherwise, the same food for thought, which should have been digested long before, will be regurgitated over and over. Begin the exchange with an agreement to listen to grievances for five minutes, say, and then to work on resolutions for ten.

5. Develop your change-the-subject skills. Before emotion spills over into irretrievable evidence such as tears or profanity or physical acts, gently shift the subject to a safer topic. Listen intently to what is being said and then pick up one word and phrase and use it to move to safer, more neutral ground.

A good way to practice such skills is to take two totally unrelated words and try to build a verbal bridge between them. Try it while watching sitcoms on TV. Tune in to an argument one character is starting. Then, isolate a word or phrase in that argument. Mute the sound and use the word or phrase to transition to more neutral, emotion-soothing ground.

Managing Energy

A trait that appears repeatedly in the lists of leadership characteristics is "energy." Famous leaders are not necessarily in good health—witness F.D.R. on crutches and J.F.K. in constant back pain—but they can be described as forceful personalities, high-energy people to whom others are drawn like iron shavings to a magnificent magnet.

In *The Biology of Success* (New York: Little, Brown & Co., 2000), Dr. Bob Arnot cites mental energy and positive thought as the two traits that characterize successful individuals. Asserting that you can retrain your brain and stop defeatist thinking, Arnot advocates high-protein foods that lead to optimistic thinking.

A Shakespearean Strategy

Tricks of the Trade

Five hundred years ago, Shakespeare had a character implore a friend, "Laugh me out of myself." Often, we can tap into energy we didn't even know we had, simply by getting up and *doing* something. Ideally, that "something" will be exercise—even if it's only walking around your office or apartment or lifting the fax machine if you don't have weights handy. Ironically, the expenditure of energy on exercise gives us *more* energy. Talking to a good friend or admired colleague can re-energize us as well. And so can the decision not to fritter away our energies on petty concerns.

Refuse to Be Insulted

When other people make deliberate or inadvertent rude remarks, you can choose to be deeply wounded by them and consequently mentally enervated. Or you can choose to shrug them off, perhaps even laugh about the circumstances and consequently experience greater mental energy. These two real-world examples will show you what we mean.

Moments before an important staff conference began, Rose walked over to Pam and admired the outfit she was wearing. Those who overheard the remark were surprised, as was Pam, for the two women were known as avowed enemies. Rose's next comment, though, suddenly explained the seeming compliment. In the sweetest of tones, Rose oozed, "I wish I could wear cheap clothes as well as you do."

Pam had two choices. She could have regarded the comment as an insult and responded in kind or she could have acted as if the comment were sincere. She chose not to take the offense.

"Oh, but you *do*," she insisted.

On a similar note is the tale of a society matron who had a rather crude guest at her table one evening. She watched him spear the meat on his plate with a fork. Holding it up in her direction, he demanded to know, "Is this pig?"

Quietly and sweetly, she asked a question in return. "To which end of the fork are you referring?" The resulting laughter, including that from the fork-holder, restored sparkle to the evening.

Try These Tips

1. Get the unpleasant tasks out of the way early so they don't drain your energy the whole day long. To quote Mark Twain, "If you have to swallow a frog, don't stare at it too long!" Even if you can't complete the entire project in one early-morning block, you can make considerable progress. And you'll feel better the rest of the day, knowing that you're progressing toward the end of a least-

favored task. (Share this frog-swallowing technique with your team as well.)

2. Engage in a five-minute luxury at least once a day. Tell yourself, "I deserve this!" And convince yourself that it's the truth. And, should you find your staff luxuriating, think, "They deserve it" before thinking, "They're goofing off."

3. If you didn't get rid of weeds, flowers would have no room to grow. List all the emotional "weeds" in your life—people or practices or papers or precepts that prevent the flowers of productivity from blooming. Vow to eliminate (or spend less emotional energy on) one weed a month.

4. Bothered by energy-ebbing headaches? Apply ice to your temples the next time you're in the middle of one. And if you feel another coming on, apply heat.

5. Once an hour—if yours is a fixed-position job—stand, stretch, move around, or take a break. Physical activity is an instant energizer.

Managing People

More than 85 years ago, an advertisement appeared in the *Saturday Evening Post* (January 2, 1915). Titled "The Penalty of Leadership," it offers an insightful look into the pain and the pleasure of dealing with others in the workplace.

> In every field of human endeavor, he that is first must perpetually live in the white light of publicity. ... Whether the leadership be vested in a man or in a manufactured product, emulation and envy are ever at work. In art, in literature, in music, in industry, the reward and the punishment are always the same.
>
> The reward is widespread recognition; the punishment fierce denial and detraction. When a man's work becomes a standard for the whole world, it also becomes a target for the shafts of the envious few. If his work is merely mediocre, he will be left severely alone. If he achieves a masterpiece, it will set a million tongues a-wagging. Jealousy does not protrude its forked tongue at the artist who produces a commonplace painting.

Whatsoever you write, or paint or play or sing or build, no one will strive to surpass or slander you unless your work be stamped with the seal of genius.

Long, long after a great work or a good work has been done, those who are disappointed or envious continue to cry out that it cannot be done. Spiteful little voices in the domain of art were raised against our own Whistler as a mountebank long after the big world had acclaimed him its greatest artistic genius.

Multitudes flocked to Bayreuth to worship at the musical shrine of Wagner while the little group of those whom he had dethroned and displaced argued angrily that he was no musician at all. The little world continued to protest that Fulton could never build a steamboat while the big world flocked to the riverbanks to see his boat steam by.

The leader is assailed because he is a leader and the effort to equal him is merely added proof of that leadership. Failing to equal or to excel, the follower seeks to deprecate and to destroy, but only confirms once more the superiority of that which he strives to supplant. There is nothing new in this. It is as old as the world and as old as the human passions: envy, fear, greed, ambition, and the desire to surpass. And it all avails nothing.

If the leader truly leads, he remains the leader. Master poet, master painter, master workman—each in his turn is assailed and each holds his laurels through the ages. That which is good or great makes itself known, no matter how loud the clamor of denial. That which deserves to live, lives.

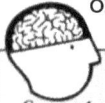

No doubt, you will find some of these sentiments as true today as they were in 1915. Others, perhaps, have undergone change with time. Two facts, though, come through loud and clear: leadership is no easy task—and people's emotions make the task even harder.

A Heavenly Tip

Smart Managing It's been pointed out that both the important prophets as well as those of lesser stature can be found in the Sistine Chapel ceiling. Michelangelo distinguished between them, though. While both sets of pro-phets have cherubs whispering in their ears, only the major prophets are listening.

As a manager of people, you can develop strong relationships with very little effort and no money at all. Just listen deeply and sincerely.

Try These Tips

1. Develop a sensitivity to body language. Read some books on the subject if you need to. The really good *readers* of this language can spot sparks long before they turn into fires. The really good *speakers* of this language ensure congruity between their words and their actions.

2. Pledge to acquire more and better people-skills. In part, this may mean letting go of slights—intended or assumed. You can manage your reactions to people who seem determined to get under your skin. (Watch how other people handle them.) Heed the results of a 20-year study from the University of London: failing to control your reactions to stressful events and people is a more dangerous risk factor for cancer and heart disease than smoking or a high-cholesterol diet.

3. It's true there are some who wear their hearts on their sleeve. But the majority of people you encounter each day are carrying emotions around inside. Although you cannot tell by looking who has just lost a child to SIDS or who is in the middle of a difficult divorce or who has just been diagnosed with a life-threatening disease, it's safe to assume people have problems. (Sometimes the more difficult the person, the most difficult the problem she carries.) Restrain your natural, and sometimes even justifiable, impulses toward sarcasm or impatience. Self-talk before talking. Try repeating the popular line, "There but for the grace of God go I," just prior to uttering damaging remarks.

4. Pride yourself on your maturity. Tell yourself you are bigger than the problem or the person causing it. Don't let others drag you down to their level of unprofessionalism.

5. According to a new study by Christine Pearson of the Kenan-Flagler Business School of the University of North Carolina at Chapel Hill ("Workplace Incivility: The Target's

Eye View," reprinted with permission), when managers act rudely:

- 53% of their employees lose hours of productive time worrying about "what will happen next time?"
- 46% consider changing jobs
- 37% report feeling less committed to the organization
- 22% "get even" by deliberately contributing less
- 12% quit their jobs to avoid the perpetrator.

How Much Are You Managing to Manage?

To lead well, you have to manage well. Apart from the technical knowledge you need to get the job done, you need other kinds of knowledge if you intend to successfully manage yourself, processes, and the people involved in the processes.

Understanding the range of stress, from distress to eustress, helps you maximize its potential and minimize its damage. You owe it to your followers to acquire this understanding. No matter how much you already know, there is always more to learn.

Don't be like the student at Princeton who met Einstein at one of the teas that were held each year so that students and faculty could socialize. Einstein was teaching there at the time and probably had not achieved the worldwide acclaim he was to know in subsequent years. The young woman approached him and asked what he did.

"I have devoted myself to the study of physics," the scientist replied.

"Really?" the young woman asked, surprise evident in her wide-eyed response. "*I* finished physics in one semester!" she boldly proclaimed.

The same advice holds for acquiring new time-management techniques, chief among them the ability to prioritize the many demands that are made upon your management/leadership time. You can always learn more.

Some would argue the most critical of all the things you manage is emotions. Current research is showing that emotion management is a requisite for business success.

Others would argue for putting energy management at the top of the list of leadership abilities. If you think about it, you'd probably have a hard time identifying a leader who appeared listless, lethargic, unenthusiastic, and/or tired all the time. Typically, leaders evince a vitality that draws others to them. You can achieve and sustain this vitality with attention to your physical well-being and with attention to the attitude you project.

Finally, continuously add to your log of people-management skills. Whenever you see a technique that works well, add it to your repertoire. Be a constant hunter. You'll find approaches worth emulating all around you—not just in the workplace. Commit to refining all your management skills. Life is easier when you do.

Manager's Checklist for Chapter 5

❏ Acquire new coping strategies. The old ones won't work as well as they once did.

❏ Ask yourself and your staff the questions that reveal how seriously burnout may be impacting you.

❏ Get professional help, if necessary, to lower the percentage of illnesses related to stress—as high as 90% by some estimates.

❏ Develop some lightening-up activities for the workplace.

❏ Help employees feel they have greater external control.

❏ Make change more acceptable to your staff by thinking globally and acting either locally or globally, welcoming criticism, learning about the lives of those around you, using visualization techniques, repeating and rephrasing your instructions to others.

❏ Set small, medium, and large goals for the use of your time.

❏ Encourage good emotional health by forgiving mistakes, prioritizing your work, using a matrix to separate the important from the urgent, asking yourself the "T" questions

(*Today? Tomorrow? Time-independent? True* reason for the job?), allocating some time each day for future projects.

❏ If you don't already have a program in place to prevent or deal with workplace violence, take a leadership role in establishing one.

❏ Develop your powers of meta-cognition (looking at a situation from two different perspectives simultaneously).

❏ Help others establish and maintain positive attitudes.

❏ Remember that "anger" is only one letter away from "danger."

❏ Encourage optimism by building "shelf-esteems," establishing support systems, setting a time limit for listening to complaints, and developing the skill of smoothly changing the subject.

❏ Learn to laugh yourself out of yourself.

❏ Refuse to be insulted by innocent remarks and even intended barbs.

❏ Do unpleasant tasks early in the day.

❏ Indulge yourself at least once a day.

❏ Get rid of the "weeds" that bring you down.

❏ Engage in more physical activity.

❏ Develop your listening skills and your ability to read body language.

❏ Read to find ways to control your negative reactions to stressful events and people.

❏ Consider what others may have to deal with before you respond with sarcasm.

❏ Don't lower yourself to the unkind tactics others may employ.

❏ Know the consequences of rude behavior.

The Leader as Communicator

"Leaders who are inarticulate make us all uneasy." This assertion by the former head of the American Management Association, James Hayes, is echoed in the words of Robert Reich, former Secretary of Labor. "To be a leader," he maintains, "is to communicate powerfully."

It's been said that when Cicero spoke, men marveled. When Caesar spoke, however, men marched. Your words must do more than make others marvel at your wordsmithing or oratorical abilities. They must move people to action. Exercise your verbal power as well as your other powers.

What are the elements that constitute such power? They're fairly easy to determine.

Just think of the most powerful, the most persuasive, the most literally influential leader you know. Then identify the qualities that contribute to her success.

Speaking

Many believe your oral communication skills are the best predictor of your managerial success. It's not enough to know how to do your job. You have to connect on a personal level with dozens of other people—your staff, your customers, your managers, people in other departments, people in the community, people in the media, and so on. Typically, those connections are made through the spoken word.

The K-I-N-D Technique

Arrogant leaders assume that because they've been using words from infancy onward, they need no further instruction on the communication process. Nothing could be further from the truth. The best communicators improve their techniques until the day they retire. Imitate their behavior. You'll find your job and your life made easier if you do.

When you encounter a difficult person—and the business world is filled with them so you will, sooner or later—use the K-I-N-D Technique.

- Begin by extending a **K**ind word or thought to the other person.
- Continue with an **I**nquiry. Ask about the person's intentions or hopes or expectations. Ask open-ended, probing questions in order to get to the heart of the matter.
- A **N**ew effort is next required from you. There's little point in interacting with the difficult person in the same way you've always interacted with her. (You've heard the definition of "insanity," we suspect: "doing the same thing over and over and expecting different results.") For the exchange to get better, you have to try a new way of working with her.
- Finally, be **D**efinite. Don't be like the two friends who meet unexpectedly on the street and assure one another, "We have to get together one of these days." That day will probably never come around unless they make a definite date: "How about next Sunday for brunch?" Similarly, you'll need to specify some follow-up in order to monitor the success of the new approach you've taken.

Here's an example of how you can respond in K-I-N-D.

You: (K) Thank you, Molly, for meeting with me this morning. I know your schedule is pretty full these days.

Molly: What exactly did you want, Les?

You: I want to explore with you ways that we might work together better.

Molly: I don't have time for this.

You: (I) Well, then, just give me the answer to just one question. Do you think we're optimizing our working relationship?

Molly: What do you mean by "optimizing"?

You: I don't think we're fully playing off each other's strengths. If we were, we would be optimizing our efforts.

Molly: What are you proposing?

You: (N) For one thing, I'd like to see us avoid duplicating each other's work.

Molly: I don't think that's a problem.

You: Perhaps not for you. However, last week I called a vendor to invite her to participate in the new bid cycle and learned you'd already explored it with her.

Molly: So?

You: So that's an example of suboptimization.

Molly: So?

You: So I'm wondering if my secretary could call your secretary and just divide the calls between them.

Molly: I don't have a problem with that.

Line Up Here — *Tricks of the Trade*

Few leaders are spontaneous 100% of the time. Usually, they have prepared lines that work well in situations they've encountered before and are likely to encounter again. Some of the lines that will serve you well with difficult people when you are taking the Inquiry step follow:

"What do you think the real issue is here?"

"What would you do if you were I?"

"Have you encountered anything like this before?"

"What can we do to work better together?"

"What do you think we should do next?"

You: (D) Thanks, Molly. I'll have Sue call Chris first thing in the morning to get the new plan under way. And, Molly, know that I appreciate your willingness to work with me on this.

More Formal Presentations

If you attend to the five C's of speech preparation, you'll save yourself considerable time. You'll also provide your listeners a well-structured presentation. Follow the outline of the five C's. They'll serve you for virtually any speaking situation.

Let's run through those five C's with an example. Imagine that you've been asked to deliver a commencement address to the local high school. Jot down some ideas in relation to each "C."

Cite the Occasion. Refer to the reason why your audience and you are occupying the same time and space on this particular day. Try to unearth an interesting bit of history concerning the event or occasion.

Cite Commonalities. Show the audience that you have something in common with them. Bob Hope, for example, always began a humorous monolog with a reference to the city in which he was speaking.

Challenge the Audience. Involve your listeners by motivating them to do something. Appeal to their imaginations, to the inclination most people have to make the world a better place. Be sure to cite the benefits associated with the change you are proposing.

Cheer Them On. Sometimes a leader has more confidence in her followers' abilities than they have themselves. Express your faith in their ability to meet the challenge you have laid before them. You can do this with references to past successes or by noting their collective talents.

Conclude. Your conclusion should do more than summarize what's been said. It should ask for an informal commitment, a pledge to make a difference in their small corner of the world.

You intend your words to inform and/or inspire. Your audience, ideally, will take what you've given and actually do something with it.

Motivation

Historian Arthur Schlesinger, Jr., described John F. Kennedy with these words: "Above all, he gave the world for an imperishable moment the vision of a leader who greatly understood the terror and the hope, the diversity and the possibility, of life on this planet and who made people look beyond nation and race to the future of humanity."

In these few words are numerous clues for those interested in inspiring others. "Vision," to be sure. What other words would you choose as elemental in the verbal makeup of a leader? What things do you "greatly understand"? How can you make others "look beyond ... to the future"?

Despite what some managers believe, every-one on your staff is motivated. Now, they may not be motivated to do what you *want* them to do, but they are motivated to do something. The trick is finding out what motivates them and trying to transfer that drive to the workplace.

> **Putting the "Extra" in "Ordinary"**   Smart Managing
>
> Peter Drucker maintains that the way to get ordinary people to do extraordinary things is to develop habits of effectiveness. This slightly different slant on motivation should lead you to ask two questions: What are your personal habits of effectiveness? and What habits of effectiveness can you help others develop?

Loyalty

Think of the institutions or individuals toward whom you feel loyalty. Apart from familial ties, what makes you willing to follow such people, to support them through good and bad times?

A number of factors constitute the loyalty equation. Among them is a belief in the position the leader takes. It's not enough to make your vision known. You have to keep on making it known—not only to increase the number of converts to your cause but also to recharge the batteries of early supporters. It's this ability to inspire others to an ideal bigger and better than our own that draws hardworking volunteers to political campaigns.

In turn, when you can show you're willing to support your supporters, you'll earn their respect and their commitment. You can demonstrate your confidence in them by making the working conditions pleasant. You can also build challenge into everyday tasks. If yours is a participative management style, you're well on your way to inspiring loyalty, for everyone likes to feel her opinion is important.

Loyalty is built from a sincere interest in the lives and careers of others. When you can, provide opportunities for your followers—advancement, visibility, training, etc. Loyalty is also built from positive relationships—between you and the staff and among the staff members. When you acknowledge your staff with deserved praise, you go a long way toward developing the relationships that will determine your project's success or failure.

Make it a point to ask your staff this question: "What was the best work experience you've had in the last year?" Study their answers and then work to intensify and replicate those circumstances as widely as you can.

Expansion

Think of all the ways you influence your staff—with words, with deeds, with direct and indirect gestures. You can expand your sphere of influence by finding ways to expand your staff members. And, as they meet success with their projects, have them think of ways to expand their projects to other offices, other divisions, other industry members.

Peter Drucker once chastised executives who complain about people whose fire-in-the-belly has been quenched. The fault, he feels, lies with the manager who has made the job too small.

Engage in job-expansion and person-expansion. But know they require clear and careful communications. Follow these steps as you work to help others reach in, reach out, and reach up.

1. Make your expectations absolutely clear well in advance of the project. Invite questions and feedback. When necessary, put details in writing.
2. Make the work interesting and valuable. You don't have to do this on a daily basis, of course, but you should have long-term career development goals for each of your staff. Learn their work-related likes and dislikes and keep a few notes. Then, when opportunities arise, you can align their interests/talents with the task.
3. Motivate by expressing confidence in the employees' abilities. Find the appropriate level of difficulty. Set them up for success, not for failure.
4. Monitor periodically and provide feedback that helps them continue on the right track or get back on it.
5. Go out of your usual way to recognize their efforts. When you think about it, there are dozens of things you can do to show appreciation without spending much in the way of time or money. A handwritten note, a greeting card, a mention at a meeting, a face-to-face compliment.

    Whatever you say or do, though, make certain the

When Jelly Beans Turn to Jelly

M. Scott Myers, a motivational expert who has worked extensively to improve union-management relations, has coined a phrase: "jelly bean motivation." He uses it to refer to empty praise. By telling a true turkey tale, he cautions managers about the dangers of meaningless praise.

One Christmas a company president gave out turkeys to all employees. The next year, of course, employees expected the same reward. Before the rumblings of discontent mounted to revolution level, the president gave in and purchased another batch. But then he heard complaints that some people's turkeys weighed more than others; employees inferred that turkey size had to do with the size of their efforts. The next year, there were complaints that some people wanted roast beef instead of turkey, so a turkey administrator had to be appointed to keep all the orders straight. You're getting the picture, aren't you?

praise is sincere and specific. If you're telling all of your followers, "Great job," as you pat each of them on the back, the recognition has very little meaning. In fact, it may even insult some if you put everyone on the same level regardless of individual contributions.

Keep your rewards simple and sincere.

Involvement

The leader intent on getting ordinary people to do extraordinary things frequently asks herself questions. The time-honored five W's and one H will do the trick for you, too. Involve your followers in answering questions like these:

- *Who* would most appreciate being given this assignment?
- *What* talents does the job call for?
- *Where* might the project run into a roadblock?
- *When* do we need to report our progress?
- *Why* might our plan be rejected?
- *How* can we ensure our success?

As you obtain and record answers, keep this anonymous bit of wisdom in mind: "The infinite capacity of human beings to misunderstand one another makes our jobs and our lives far more difficult than they have to be." Strive for clarity with both your questions and their answers.

Affiliation

Ever watch citizens of a community, right after their team has won a national championship? As the news cameras pan the crowd, you'll invariably see big signs proclaiming them "#1." We all like to be associated with a triumphant force, no matter how peripheral our connection may be.

Motivating your team of followers is easy if you can think of ways to develop cohesion. Research from Frederick Herzberg and uncountable others shows money is not the primary motivator. In fact, the feeling of being part of a successful team is a more powerful drive than money for most people. We all want to feel we make a difference.

Leaders who make our efforts an important part of the big picture of success help us feel important. They go out of their way to connect us to the mission and to each other.

In reaching out to others, you indirectly reach into yourself. As Ralph Waldo Emerson noted, "It is one of the most beautiful compensations of this life that no man can sincerely try to help another without helping himself." The more overtures you make to build your team, the more win/win outcomes you're likely to have.

Ability to Think on Your Feet

Learning to think well on your feet, according to Lee Iacocca, is the best thing you can do for your career. Now, you may dis-agree—it is, after all, just one man's opinion. But you'd proba-bly agree that this skill is valuable for people in leadership positions.

Further evidence of corporate America's inter-est in this special skill can be found in the highly imi-tated Workout sessions Jack Welch has instituted at General Electric. Participants in this forum-like setting get a mental workout as demanding as

> ### Expect the Unexpected
>
> Not long ago, a senior at Dartmouth College went on an interview for a job as a product manager intern at Microsoft. The "interview" was basically a single request: "Design a full-page *Wall Street Journal* ad per-suading us to hire you." This kind of interview challenge illustrates the emphasis on quick thinking that is val-ued in employees.

the term implies. They are also encouraged to take unneces-sary work out of their jobs. And, they can work out problems together. You can adapt the following description to your own circumstances.

The manager and her subordinates convene in an off-site location. She briefly addresses her team about issues that need to be dealt with, problems that need to be solved in the weeks and months ahead. After distributing a one- or two-page outline, the manager leaves the room and doesn't return until the third day. The subordinates break into subgroups. Each tackles one part of the outline—listing complaints, proposing solutions, preparing presentations.

The manager, naturally, has no idea of what's been discussed. All she knows as she sits in front of the room on the third day is that *her* managers are there to watch the workout. The next phase of the workout session has the subgroups making proposals regarding the issues and problems. For each, the manager must make a decision. She can agree to the proposal, reject it (after listing her objections), or ask for more information by a certain date (after which she'll make the decision). That's it.

Of course, the safest thing would be to table each and every decision. But doing so would make the manager appear indecisive in the eyes of her managers. If she rejects every proposal, it's clear she is a micromanager who fears relinquishing power. And if she agrees to every proposal, she could be labeled an impractical idealist.

The sessions have proven to be highly effective on many levels, not the least of which is the hundreds of thousands of dollars saved by the ideas presented. (A variation on the Workout theme has been instituted at Intel by CEO Andy Grove.) These employee-empowering meetings reflect the demands placed on today's leaders—demands for them to think quickly and decisively.

Today's leader is constantly challenged—by employees, by her managers, by customers, by the media, by technological developments, and so on. The past no longer offers the comfort of precedent—not in today's rapidly changing climate. Just as organizations now regard themselves as highly responsive, integrated, and evolving systems, so are those who lead expected to integrate diverse elements; to respond easily, clearly, and quickly; to evolve continuously as leaders and learners.

Think of your last challenging situation, one in which others judged the rapidity and quality of your responses. How well did you handle it? If you think you could have done better, try this next time. Take a minute or two to relax your nerves and focus your mental energies *before* facing the difficult person or circumstances.

Use an exercise like the following. (You'll need to prepare it in advance and put it aside until you need it. Or, have a colleague prepare the exercise for you so you're not familiar with the "answers." Whichever advance preparation method you select, keep the exercise in a folder until you need to concentrate on an upcoming challenge.)

Think of a six-letter word, such as "carpet." Write that word with a bracket to the *left* of each letter:

[c [a [r [p [e [t.

Then think of another six-letter word, such as "muscle." The second word will be written with a bracket to the *right* of each letter:

m] u] s] c] l] e].

The challenge comes with the combination of these two words:

[c m] [a u] [r s] [p c] [e l] [t e].

Write at least 10 sets of words this way. That's the preparation phase of this exercise.

Then, just before your next tension-producing meeting or interview, concentrate on figuring out the words. By the time the meeting begins, your energies will be in the "mental" zone and not in the emotional one.

Embedded Words

Concentrating well often translates to speaking well. If you can focus less on

---

Verbal Fluidity

Tricks of the Trade

You can devise numerous other self-competitions. For example, set a timer for one minute and see if you can come up with 20 words that start with the letter "m" and pertain to management. Or, 20 four-letter words (they can't end in "s") that pertain to something in or on the body, such as "mole" or "face." Or, 20 titles that contain a woman's name, such as Beatles favorite, "Michelle, Ma Belle."

yourself and more on what the other person is saying, you may find the reply you need embedded in what you've just heard.

For example, there is a very successful real estate agent in Rochester, New York. Many years ago, when her agency was just a business plan, she met with a loan officer at a bank.

He listened patiently as she laid out the facts and figures. When she finished, he had only one question for her: "Does your husband know you're doing this?"

Most of us would have given a direct answer to this direct question. Not so this budding businesswoman. She heard the word "husband" and it led her to an associated word, "wife." And that led her to a question of her own: "Does your wife know you're asking questions like that?"

The loan officer immediately realized it was time to focus on the facts and figures and not peripheral questions of gender capability. He approved the loan immediately thereafter.

Another example comes from the world of politics. The associated terms in the following true story are "reading" and "writing."

Liz Carpenter served as press secretary in the Johnson White House. Despite her demanding duties, she managed to find time to write a book. Historian Arthur Schlesinger obtained a copy of it soon after its release and approached Carpenter one day with this backhanded compliment. "I read your book, Liz," he is reported to have said. "And it's very good. Who wrote it for you?"

Without missing a beat, Carpenter accepted the compliment and then asked a question of her own. "I'm glad you enjoyed it, Arthur," she replied. "Who read it to you?"

Definitions

People who think well on their feet usually have an arsenal of weapons to use when the war of words is being waged upon them. One technique you can use when you're under fire (friendly or otherwise) is the definition. You can employ it as a toss-back or as a lead-in. The toss-back definition sounds like this:

Challenger: I'm very concerned about a statement you made recently. You said that a popular management book was originally written for parents. Are you implying that we exhibit child-like behavior?

You: Well, let me ask: How do you define "child-like behavior"?

The lead-in definition buys you time. It allows you to segue between the question or probe given to you and your own polished reply. Here's an example:

Challenger: Why did you go into supervision in the first place?

You: I like the Latin concept of supervision. The word originally meant having a vision that was "super" or "above" the ordinary, everyday events. The idea of coordinating the efforts of many hardworking people appeals to me. I'm challenged by the prospect of overseeing their input to achieve a final output that represents the best we each have to offer.

Quotations

If you attend very carefully to the words of those who can think on their feet without putting them in their mouth, you're bound to detect a reliance on quotations. Leaders who motivate have

Double the Pleasure

You can often motivate your team by presenting them with quotations that reflect opposite viewpoints. Then, use the quotes to help the team decide on their direction.

To illustrate, let's assume you've heard some expression of doubt about a leadership project you've proposed. Present *two* quotations to your team: "An anonymous sage once remarked that we should make no small plans for small plans have no power to stir the soul. But, Mother Teresa said that we can do no great things, only small things with great love."

Then ask someone, "There is merit in both these viewpoints. But, clearly, we cannot follow both at the same time. Terry, which of these comes closer to the direction we should take with this? Should we think big? Should we adopt some of those 'big, hairy, audacious' goals author Jim Collins talks about? Or should we concentrate on doing small things with great commitment?"

taken the time to memorize several quotes that suit a variety of situations. When the admirable words of others can roll tripping-ly off your tongue and when those words are perfect for the situation, you cannot help but inspire.

If you don't have many quotes stored in your verbal repertoire, begin with short ones, such as this from author Tom Peters: "Every organization should have at least one weirdo on staff." Set a goal of adding at least one quote a month and let the quotes work for you as often as you can.

Persuasion

It's fairly easy to be labeled a persuasive person. It's much harder to earn the label of a principled persuader. History has seen the tragic outcomes of unscrupulous persuaders, such as those leaders who persuade hundreds of their followers to commit suicide. So prevalent are the malevolent that they've evoked this commentary from Albert Einstein: "The real problem is in the hearts and minds of men. It is easier to denature plutonium than to denature the evil spirit of man."

As an ethical leader, you carry numerous responsibilities on your shoulders to embody goodness and to "denature evil."

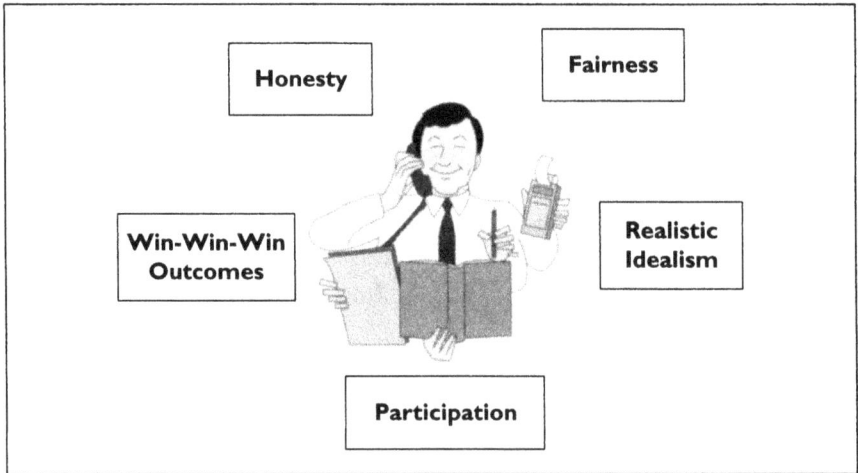

Figure 6-1. The ethical leader's responsibilities

As Figure 6-1 illustrates, the leader whose persuasiveness motivates others does so by being committed to Honesty, Fairness, Realistic Idealism, Participation, and Win-Win-Win Outcomes.

Honesty. The truth sometimes hurts. But the best leaders depend on followers who can handle the truth, who don't need sugarcoating, who are often inspired by the challenge inherent in the unvarnished truth. To cover up—no matter how well-intentioned your purpose—is to invite subsequent charges of untrustworthiness.

Fairness. Most people associate fairness with consistency. Ironically, being fair usually means *not* being consistent. Different people have different needs. When you lead, you have to walk the fine line between treating everyone with the same respect and yet responding to unique strengths and differences. When you negotiate, when you propose, and ultimately, when you persuade, make sure you're presenting a balanced picture. (The sins of omission are often as injurious as the sins of commission.)

Realistic Idealism. Another fine communication line leaders have to walk is the one separating realism and idealism. Too grandiose a vision may imply impracticality. Too realistic an assessment may strip the project of its excitement.

Participation. Leaders sometimes lead the parade. At other times, they simply march in it. Occasionally, they bring up the rear—or even clean up the debris that inevitably results when people convene. Don't make the mistake of assuming you have to do everything, just because the idea behind the project was *your* idea.

> **Shaw's Law**
>
> George Bernard Shaw wryly maintained that power does not corrupt people. "Fools," he noted, "if they get into a position of power, corrupt power." His myth-shattering message contains a caveat: when you communicate, don't sound "foolish." Use your power wisely and make it clear you're doing so. Find novel and interesting ways to repeat your message without being tiresome or power-struck.

Find ways to involve every member of your team. Share the power associated with success and share it willingly. Learn to admit, graciously, that some of your followers may be better at some things than you are. When you persuade others to follow you, do so generously.

Win/Win/Win Outcomes. We've been trained as a business community to seek win/win outcomes. Ideally, you can take your leadership team to a higher level, one at which you consider a third beneficiary. It won't take long before you're looking at every scenario in terms of three-part advantages.

Willingness to Shatter Myths

In keeping with the concept of leader as one who disturbs the status quo, we have business "radicals" like Tom Peters, for example. He asserts, "If you have gone a whole week without being disobedient, you are doing yourself and your organization a disservice." Leaders challenge us to step out of comfort zones, to replace "foolish consistency" with avant-garde thinking.

Think of some myths that surround your organization, your industry, your business community. (Aim for a list of 10.) Which of these myths would you be willing to shatter? What price would you be willing to pay for "telling it like it is"?

Writing

To quote the inimitable Yogi Berra, "You can see a lot just by observing." That's a great way to learn. Whom should you observe? Those leaders whose communication style inspires. A quick look at any major speech by any major figure will yield you numerous tips you can use in your own persuasion efforts.

Ronald Reagan, in his second inaugural address illustrates the use of *interesting statistics*:

> When the first president, George Washington, placed his hand upon the Bible, he stood less than a single day's journey by horseback from raw, untamed wilderness.

In that address, Reagan also made *comparisons and contrasts:*

> There were four million Americans in a union of 13 states.

Today we are 60 times as many in a union of 50 states.

(To create a historical perspective, Reagan also used here a "then-and-now" comparison.)

Another technique is to *emphasize shared values.* Here is an example:

> While not every American reads the Bible, for the majority of citizens, it reflects a common belief in a higher authority.

Another techniques is to *vary sentence length.* The sentence in the first Reagan quote contains 26 words; the two sentences in the second quote contain and 11 and 13. Conversely, the ineffective communicator makes every sentence virtually the same length. The powerful persuader, by contrast, understands the power of variety.

The effective communication also *uses variety in sentence structure.* For example, Reagan's first quote starts with a dependent clause. The second example uses two short declarative sentences, but with one beginning with an adverb. Dull communicators start every sentence the same way, usually with a noun-verb combination. Powerful communicators refuse to do so.

Clear communicators *use transitions.* The word "today" is one of those words that serve as verbal glue, connecting what went before to what follows. If you're not employing such words, your sentences probably sound disjointed. In all likelihood, you lack a smooth, seamless flow from one thought to another.

In just four sentences, you have six techniques that work to make your words more memorable, your appeal more persuasive. Commit to studying other speeches once a month and record the results of your analyses.

Manager's Checklist for Chapter 6

❏ Improve your communication skills by learning about and trying techniques, such as the K-I-N-D technique (*K*ind, *I*nquiry, *N*ew, *D*efinite) and, for more formal presentations, the Five C's (*C*ite the occasion, *C*ite commonalities, *C*hallenge the audience, *C*heer them on, *C*onclude).

❑ Have prepared lines for unexpected but anticipated situations.

❑ Develop habits of effectiveness for yourself and your team.

❑ Inspire loyalty by drawing others to a vision, supporting your supporters, providing opportunities, learning about your staff, and encouraging expansion.

❑ Be careful about using "jelly bean motivation," which can backfire.

❑ Use the five W's and one H when you want to involve others.

❑ Know and use the power of affiliation.

❑ Learn to think on your feet by expecting the unexpected, instituting Workout sessions, engaging in exercises designed to increase verbal fluidity, listening for embedded words, and using definitions and quotations.

❑ Ensure that your persuasive efforts reflect honesty, fairness, realistic idealism, and chance for participation. Design them to yield win/win/win outcomes.

❑ Shatter myths that need to be reexamined or perhaps replaced.

❑ Study the speeches of outstanding persuaders. Identify the stylistic devices that work for others and make them work for you.

7

The Leader as Power Distributor

Unfortunately, in the minds of many people, "power" has certain negative overtones. For some, the word connotes a Machiavellian twist. Power can be bad, yes, but power can also be good. Used wisely, power can translate goals into reality for the benefit of several communities. Used for self-aggrandizement, power may benefit the unscrupulous leader for a short time but could destroy trust and morale for a long time.

The Leader's Use of Power

America is a nation that has rebelled against power. We cherish our independence and resist those who seek to wrest it from us. Our government was established to balance the uses of power; similar checks and balances exist in virtually every organization. Labor unions, as an example, protect the rights of employees against powerful management forces. Such entities as grievance committees or Equal Employment Opportunity (EEO) committees function the same way.

Until quite recently, we've looked with disfavor upon those hungry for power as individuals we had to protect ourselves against. (Megalomania, after all, is a mental disorder.) Typically, those driven by power are viewed as self-serving individuals who manipulate others in order to achieve their own ends.

Like so many other things, though, "power" is simply a word. How you interpret that word makes all the difference. You can use power to benefit a great many others or you can unethically use power to benefit yourself alone.

The most successful leaders use power wisely and well. They not only optimize the advantages of having power; they've also learned to share their power with others.

When you give your subordinates some control in decisions that affect them, they're bound to feel appreciated, valued, and satisfied. They're more likely to demonstrate loyalty, make contributions, and operate on the basis of pride. They're *less* likely to quit, perform poorly, or subvert your plans.

One of the simpler ways to share power is to create a composite agenda. In other words, instead of having your own agenda as the singular force behind the mission, ask others what their own goals are for the project. Then, fashion a statement of purpose that reflects all the best intentions.

Defining Power

Power does not flow to invisible people. As your ideas gain more and more visibility, more and more power will be accorded you. How well do you use and share that power? As you begin to rethink your attitudes toward power, consider this from Harvard professor John Kotter: "From my own observations, I suspect that a large number of managers—especially the young, well-educated ones—perform significantly below their potential because they do not understand the dynamics of power and because they have not nurtured and developed the instincts needed to effectively acquire and use power" (John Kotter, "Power, Dependence, and Effective Management," *Harvard Business Review*, July-August 1977).

Using this definition of "power"—"the judicious use of influence to get things done through other people"—you should be able to calm your qualms about acquiring and using power. If you don't, according to Kotter, you'll probably perform below your potential.

What are the dynamics of power and how can you nurture and develop your instincts for using power for positive results?

Well, when you think about it, you've been doing exactly this for a very long time. The process is referred to in the old sayings, "One hand washes the others" and "You scratch my back and I'll scratch yours." If you understand these colloquial expressions, you understand relationships built on power.

When you help others, you do so for unselfish reasons, of course. But the fact remains that—having gone out of your way for someone—you have developed an indebtedness. You know that when you need a favor, that person will probably be willing to go out of his way for you. You engage in such behaviors with friends and family members. Doing so with business associates does not change the mutually beneficial nature of the process.

> ### Force Could Be Your Waterloo
>
> Napoleon once observed, "There are but two powers in the world: the sword and the mind. In the long run, the sword is always beaten by the mind." In other words, you can compel or impel others to do your bidding. But coercion seldom works. When it does, the results are usually not long-lasting. By contrast, you can excite others, encourage them, influence them through intrinsic motivation. When you do, you capture their minds and their loyalty in the process.

As a final example of the need to let go your dislike of certain words, take the following test (reprinted with permission from *Principled Persuasion: Influence with Integrity, Sell with Standards*, Rochester, NY: CPD Press, 1999, pp. 355-356). Just answer "Agree" or "Disagree" for each statement.

1. We should be adaptable when unforeseen events occur. _____

2. One change always leaves indentations upon which to build another change. _____

3. In the beginning, problems are easy to cure but hard to diagnose; with the passage of time, having gone unrecognized and unattended, they become easy to diagnose but hard to cure.   _____

4. A workplace that is used to freedom is more easily managed by its own employees than by any other arrangement.   _____

5. A wise influencer must always tread the path of great men and women and should imitate those who have excelled.   _____

6. People who least rely on luck alone will be the most successful.   _____

7. Success is a combination of opportunity and ability.   _____

8. Most people have no faith in new things until they have been proved by experience.   _____

9. If you have to beg others to fulfill a mission, you are destined to fail.   _____

10. If you are respected, you will be secure, honored, and successful.   _____

11. Things that come easily are hard to maintain. Things that are hard-won are easier to maintain.   _____

12. A leader who thinks more about his own interest than about yours, who seeks his own advantage for everything he does, will never be a good leader, for others will never be able to trust him.   _____

13. In order to keep employees loyal, managers must honor them by sharing both distinctions and duties.   _____

How'd you do? Count the number of "Agree" answers you have.

Was it more than six? If so, you could be labeled "Machiavellian" in your thinking, because these 13 slightly paraphrased statements are taken directly from *The Prince* by Niccolo

Macchiavelli. For the last 500 years, the author's name has been synonymous with words like "duplicity" and "deceit." Yet this is a misunderstanding of much of his message. All of the ideas noted above are consistent with the best management thinking today, from Deming to Drucker to Blanchard and many others.

M-Powers

Few business words have been used as much in the last decade as "empowerment." You're probably tired of hearing the word, but you shouldn't be tired of seeing the results of empowering actions. You can share power with your subordinates by having them turn *wishful* thinking into *workable* thinking. Success with empowering depends, as does nearly everything else in the world of business, on effective communications. Simply ask your team members, one at a time, what they would do differently if they had the power to do it.

Then ask what level of empowerment they would like to have in converting this wish to reality. For example, if someone says he'd like to be more involved with benchmarking, show him the various "In" levels available—inform, investigate, intend, initiate, independent—and ask him to select one on which to operate.

Level 1. *Inform* The follower basically gathers information about benchmarking and shares it with the leader.

Level 2. *Investigate* The follower basically gathers information but also tells the leader what options or courses of action are available.

Level 3. *Intend* The follower does what's done in Levels 1 and 2 but goes beyond to explain which of the options he would follow.

Level 4. *Initiate* The follower starts and stops the project virtually on his own, simply keeping the leader apprised of progress at various stages.

Level 5. *Independent* The follower essentially works on his own at this level. Because the leader knows him well and trusts him and his work explicitly, there is little need for informing or getting the approval required in the other levels.

Give consideration to the three M-words discussed in the following sections. They'll broaden the scope of your empowering efforts. They'll also enable your followers to develop self-direction and entrepreneurial behaviors.

Mentoring

Given the power structures most organizations have set up, some people invariably feel disenfranchised. One way to empower them, to assure them they have as many opportunities as anyone else, is to have a mentoring program. Such efforts validate. They develop confidence. They bring out talents team members may not even have known they possessed.

When self-doubt keeps followers from achieving their potential, mentoring puts doubt in a secondary position so ability can take a primary stand. You have many choices when it comes to

Questions to Ask

Good mentoring programs don't just happen. They're planned. And part of the planning inevitably involves asking questions. Among the ones you should consider are these:

- What criteria do we need to establish?
- How do we recruit people for the program?
- What rewards exist for the mentor?
- How much time will mentoring take?
- Who will administer the program?
- How will conflicts be handled, should they arise?
- What responsibilities will the mentor have?
- Should friendship between the two parties be encouraged?
- How do we match mentor and protégé?
- Should we pair women with women and men with men or doesn't gender matter?
- Should job function be considered in setting up the mentoring program?
- How should we evaluate the mentoring program?
- What are our objectives?
- What expectations do the various stakeholders have?

instituting such a program. You can make it formal or informal, short-term or long-term, single-mentored or multiple-mentored. Whatever choices you make, however, keep in mind the primary purpose of mentoring: to set up a support system that helps people learn, grow, and contribute.

The trust factor is an important one in the mentoring equation. The mentor can engender trust by keeping the promises he makes and by showing chinks in the seemingly impenetrable armor of success. If he, for example, acknowledges mistakes he made in his career, he will seem less formidable to the protégé. Too, the mentor must not neglect the mentoring relationship. To do so defeats the whole purpose behind this empowerment effort.

The protégé needs to be honest, too, in admitting fears or doubts or concerns. Otherwise, it will be difficult for the mentor to zero in on needed improvements. And, the protégé will have to prove that the advice and feedback given are not being dumped into a black hole. Showing results will assure the mentor that his time is well-spent.

Management

As a manager, you manage many things, among them people, procedures, and processes. As an empowering leader, you can help others manage those things and many others. In the process, of course, they will become even more competent and even more recognized. Are you a secure leader? If so, you'll take pride in the accolades your team receives. As Colonel Larry Donnithorne, author of *The West Point Way of Leadership*, remarks,

Henry's Hubris

Smart Managing

Students of American automotive history know that at one point in Ford's history, Henry Ford appointed himself as the maker of all decisions—large and small. Believe it or not, he actually had corporate spies skulking around, trying to catch his managers in the act of making decisions by themselves. Needless to say, productivity declined, as did morale.

Profits plummeted as well. Not until 15 years later did the company make a profit and the managers make their own decisions.

"Effective leaders want the best, most competent people around them—and are not threatened by them" (Sallie Motsch, "Think Gray," *Incentive*, April 1995, p. 60).

Help your followers move into management roles and leadership positions—if only on a limited basis. You can do this in part by delegating responsibility to them. Follow these five steps to ensure ideal results.

1. *Determine the task.* Delegating is not dumping. And, it is not simply sharing the workload. The best delegators begin with a careful depiction of tasks. Some tasks should never be delegated—those dealing with confidentiality, for example, or with certain safety or personnel issues. When you delegate, you need to think about the tasks—whether or not *you* want to do them—that will most help others grow. When you share your managerial or leadership power, you do so in the belief that others profit from it and will establish power of their own, in time.

2. *Match it to talent.* Once you've determined which tasks should be delegated, then you need to align each task with the talents and/or interests of those you want to empower. "Matching," of course, requires advising and getting consent.

3. *Set the parameters with the delegate.* You have to discuss and decide upon issues of authority and responsibility with your delegate. You also have to determine deadlines and other parameters surrounding the task or project you're delegating.

4. *Monitor periodically.* It's not enough to simple turn over a task to a follower. You need to be there when he has questions and be there when he has answers. Set up a regular schedule of checking in to ensure progress is being made in the agreed-upon direction.

5. *Reward effort.* Success, of course, is its own reward. But, upon completion of the delegated task, you should set aside time to review lessons learned—both positive and negative lessons. This is the time, also, to show appreciation of the delegate's efforts. You can do this simply, by expressing your grati-

tude, or more formally, by writing a letter or commendation for the delegate's efforts or by inviting him to a victory lunch. Many other gestures of appreciation are possible, of course.

Mindsets

"Whatever you can do or dream you can—begin it. Boldness has genius, power, and magic in it." Goethe's words reflect the mindset necessary for being power-hungry and for satisfying that hunger. You probably have in your team of followers a few members uncomfortable with acquiring power. Don't foist it upon them. But work with such people to expand their confidence in their own power.

Begin by assigning small tasks, particularly those on Levels 1 and 2 (Inform and Investigate). Once the person has demonstrated interest and success, encourage a higher level of involvement on another, more challenging project. In time, they'll come to know the boldness power of which Goethe speaks.

Knowledge Is Power

It's been said that if we only knew what we know, we could be three times more productive than we are. Leaders who selfishly regard knowledge as power believe the more knowledge they keep to themselves, the more power they will have. Ethical leaders are willing to share knowledge, just as they are willing to share power. Empower others by creating a knowledge network. You're creative enough to find new ways of doing this, but here are a few to get you started.

Create a Skill Bank. No one knows it all. To help those with a vacuum in their knowledge banks—and that would be everyone in the organization—learn from those who have that particular vacuum already filled, you can create a skill bank. To illustrate, assume John is extremely knowledgeable about creating spreadsheets. Mary, who is extremely knowledgeable about many things but not about spreadsheets, would look in a directory under the words "Spreadsheets." There, she would find John's name and phone number or e-mail address.

> ⚠️ **CAUTION!**
>
> ### For Those Who Don't Just Say No
>
> Not everyone has learned to "just say no." To have your skill bank program succeed, you have to protect those who don't know how to decline excessive requests. You'll find numerous ways to set protection parameters around such individuals. For example, you could make it a stipulation that no one person can answer more than three requests a month.
>
> But think ahead to the problems that might arise and have solutions ready in the form of regulations to which bank "depositors" and "withdrawers" must subscribe.

Who sets up such a directory? You do ... with a few provisos. People calling upon the subject matter experts (SMEs) have to realize their requests will be accommodated at the SMEs' discretion. And, in a show of cooperation and fairness, each person tapping an SME is expected to have his name listed in the directory as an SME of a different sort.

It doesn't take long to set up or update such a directory. But the results are remarkable in terms of uniting knowledge-haves and knowledge-have-nots.

Keep a Notebook of Conference/Training Results. You can demonstrate your leadership in another way. Institute a notebook—electronic or just plain paper—that contains a one-page summary of training or conferences coworkers have attended. The larger the organization, the greater the opportunity for savings—of time, money, and energy.

E-Mail New Learnings Weekly. You can keep colleagues electronically informed on a weekly basis of changes in corporate policy or changes in the industry. Think about the knowledge you most value in terms of successfully managing or leading a given project. Ask others what they most value. Then give a tip a week to subscribers eager to empower themselves with knowledge. You can also include quotes from leaders in the field, relevant statistics, etc. Keep it short, though, because everyone's already overworked and overinformed.

Create or Update the Web Site. If your organization doesn't already have a Web site, work to create one. If it does, work to update it with, for example, position papers or short articles from employees at various levels of the company.

Request Interviews. Invite senior managers in your firm to share their best practices. Have them discuss vision, mission, and strategy. Ask them how they've come to know what they know. Uncover the secrets of their success. Learn what initiatives are under way and what direction the organization is heading in. Then distribute this knowledge to team members. If they tell you they profited from it, share it with a wider circle.

You can also request interviews with experts outside your organization. Use the same process you'd use with in-house experts. As a variation on this knowledge theme, involve the least powerful among your followers. You could interview *them*, or have them join you in the interviewing, or have them distribute the knowledge you acquire.

> **Drowning or Starved?**
>
> There's a difference between *information* and *knowledge*. In the words of John Naisbitt, author of *Megatrends*, "We are drowning in information but starved for knowledge." Make certain that the ideas you share are relevant, that they fall into the category of "need to know" more often than "nice to know." Don't inundate with facts. Rather, provide knowledge that's usable, practical, and applicable.

Power Politics

There is a power derived from anticipating next moves. It involves the kind of forecasting that hockey legend Wayne Gretsky alluded to when he spoke of knowing where the puck will be. Moving from the hockey rink to the ring of people who surround you, you can develop similar forecasting ability. But you will have to study people and remain sensitive to words that are not spoken, attitudes not overtly expressed, behaviors that may not be what they seem.

How sensitive are you to the fears your followers may have? Do you know what makes key players tick? Do you know what turns certain decision-makers on and off? Do you know how to bring out the best in the worst?

You may not like it. You may want to deny it. But the fact remains that handling the politics of your job is critical to success. Overcome your dislike of this essential element by doing the following:

1. Follow the grapevine. Tune in to what's being said unofficially. Learn what the rumors are, what the concerns are, what the projections are. You'll learn who's in the "in group" and who's on the outs, so to speak.
2. Determine who the power brokers are and try to infiltrate that group. If you do so to advance your cause rather than to self-aggrandize, then you needn't feel any discomfort at all about doing this.
3. Take deserved credit for yourself and your team. Speak up when it seems you're being overlooked.
4. Avoid self-damning prefaces, such as "This will probably seem like a dumb question, but ...." Also avoid reminding others of mistakes you've made or unsuccessful projects you've been part of.
5. Use underhanded behavior as a last resort. Fight fire, started by the unscrupulous power mongers, with the same kind of fire only when you've exhausted other means.
6. Know that there is power behind the throne. Treat those in support positions with the same respect you accord to their managers.
7. Be professional in acknowledging the merits of competitors but don't make your own efforts seem less important than theirs.
8. Learn the meetings at which important decisions are made and try to attend as many as you can.
9. Develop loyalty in your subordinates through sincere recognition of their contributions.
10. Study those who can blow their own horn without sounding raucous. Imitate their verbal behaviors.

You may hope to avoid the political game altogether and just do your job. You may wish to work in a place where politics doesn't exist. Unfortunately, choosing to hope rather than deal

What You Know and Who You Know

You've probably heard it said that technical ability is 90% of any job and the other half is politics. As a leader, you're **Smart Managing** required to do less manual labor and more mental labor. In part, that labor depends on knowing other people and influencing them to accomplishment.

To get cooperation through political influence, you have to start with a positive mindset. If you think of politics in negative terms, if you disdain those who play the political game, then you'll never be a power player in the great game of business politics.

with reality won't help you get the credit you deserve. Avoiding politics translates to leading less effectively. All things being equal, the leader with political clout achieves his agenda more easily than the leader without.

Of course, there are those who play the game unfairly. But you can use specific tactics for dealing with such people. You can learn to go around them, above them, below them, and through them when necessary. Keep your eyes open for deceptive practices. When you suspect them or spot them, tell the person who plays "dirty" politics of your observation. You can often counter the ploys merely by recognizing them.

Too, you can try the now-it's-your-turn approach. Whenever you're asked to do something that feels like a concession, do it with this proviso, "Fine. I'm happy to do it ... this time. Next time, I'll expect you to reciprocate."

Political Campaigns

Success at work is often a matter of having a plan and following it. You probably think of planning in terms of short-term and long-term results or operational and strategic details. But there are other plans you can make as well. For example, you can plan to overcome resistance. Doing so will help you exert greater power by understanding and then winning over the various personality types who populate the workplace "jungle." Plan a campaign that places you in the forefront of those who know how to win influence with unfriendly people, a few of whom are described as follows.

Owls. Every team needs people who are knowledgeable. Ideally, your smart followers are not owls—smart people with an attitude. Owls can make team life difficult, for they always seem to have the answer, often insisting it's the only answer. While their attitude might tempt you to keep owls off your team, they usually have valuable input. How to cope with this duality? Try one (or more) of these methods.

1. Limit the amount of time the owl expounds. Otherwise, he will dominate every meeting and, in the process, intimate others who just may have equally good ideas to contribute.
2. On occasion, ask the owl to submit a detailed analysis of the course of action he's recommending. Distribute it in advance of the meeting Then, when the group convenes, hold a question-and-answer period so everyone can respond to the points made and express an opinion about the viability of the proposal. Let the majority rule in terms of deciding whether or not to proceed with the owl's plan.
3. Ask the owl to mentor a new or inexperienced member. That way, you can acknowledge his expertise and let others profit directly from it.
4. Invite the owl to only selected meetings, those at which you want to hear him elaborate on his point of view.

Lambs. These are team members who are acquiescent, passive, and noncontributing. Certainly, you respect their wish to remain in the background. However, you know that high-impact teams are composed of fully participating members.

It Takes All Kinds

Value each and every team member. There's extensive research that shows teams made up of only intellectual types are not as productive as teams composed of people with various skills and abilities. Find an article illustrating this and cite it at the beginning of your next meeting. You'll be directly expressing appreciation of diversity. Indirectly, you'll be letting the owl know that the sum is greater than the contribution of any one of the "parts." Aim for a blend of creativity, practicality, and knowledge in your team make-up.

Lambs often have good ideas to contribute, but—for whatever reason—simply prefer not to. You have several choices in dealing with lambs. Try them all until you find one that works best.

1. Quietly praise them (and not necessarily during the meeting) when they do make a contribution.
2. Pair them with more vocal members so they can offer suggestions via the second person if need be.
3. Speak to the introverted person in private, explaining that you value their input and would like to see and hear more of it.
4. Occasionally, ask for ideas in a different forum. For example, brainstorming doesn't always have to be a verbal exchange, with ideas written on a flip chart. You can request individual, recorded responses by using a format such as the Seven's Heaven technique.

Hyenas. As the name implies, hyenas may have joined your cause for the social prospects it affords, rather than out of a true commitment to the ideals you espouse. Every group of followers needs socializing, of course, but not if it jeopardizes accomplishment.

Seven's Heaven

TRICKS OF THE TRADE

When you need to energize a team or when a group seems to have encountered brick walls in the brain, you can generate workable suggestions in just a few minutes. Clearly state the problem or issue that needs to be resolved. Post it on chart paper if you can. Ask people to write down seven possible solutions. Then, begin a round-robin process of calling on one person at a time to share their ideas while someone records them on chart paper.

If they hear someone ahead of them giving a solution they had written, then they have to think of a new one quite quickly. If they absolutely can't, simply ask if they want to pass and move on to the next person. Once the list is complete, ask for volunteers (at least two) to leave the room with the list. When they return 10 to 15 minutes later, they'll share their top five choices. The team will vote again to reduce the list to the most-favored selection.

If you find the hyenas disrupting your serious intentions, you can always:

1. Have a prepared line that will cut short the hyena's jokes. You can start the meeting, for example, with a statement like this: "We're meeting today for only 20 minutes. And ... we have to reach a decision regarding the procurement policy. This means, John, that you'll have to save your humorous remarks until the end of the meeting. You can entertain people as they're walking out, not as they're working out this problem."
2. Use body language to discourage the hyena when the repartee is excessive. Frown, or shake your head, or hold your hand out in a stop-traffic gesture.
3. Appoint a topic monitor so you don't have to come across as the "heavy" every time the hyena begins his revelry. The monitor will have full authority to redirect discussion to the meeting's purpose.
4. Issue general, gentle reminders of the importance of task or mission accomplishment. This way, it won't seem as if you are always picking on the hyena alone.

Lions. Some followers are definitely wannabe leaders. They need to be in charge, to take control, to exert their influence whether or not they've been officially named as leader of a given project. The strength of lions has to be maximized, yes. But the other followers should not be terrorized by that strength. Achieving the right balance in working with lions is not easy but you can harness their aggression without alienating them. Here are some possibilities.

1. Share the power, for finite periods of time, with such individuals. Appoint the lion to take charge of a special project once in a while.
2. Stand up to the lion. Let him know more than one king can rule the jungle and that you're not content to assume a supportive role.
3. Try holding a meeting where you, the lion, and several

other members of the team talk about his behavior. There's strength in numbers and it may be that the only strength your lion will respect is the strength comparable to his own.

4. As a last resort, you can always put the lion in complete charge of a project on which he'll work in isolation, periodically reporting (preferable in writing) to the team.

Queen Bees. Queen bees simply expect drones to take care of the details that enable them to sit with power upon the throne. The queen bee doesn't do his or her share of the work but is quite willing to accept the praise derived from successful projection completion.

To offset the sting of the queen bee's behavior, try the following:

1. Make equitable and public distributions of the work. Without sounding accusatory and without singling the bee out, you could have a short speech accompany the distributions. To illustrate, you might say, "You all know how much we depend on one another. When one person fails to complete his assignment, the whole team suffers. So I'm counting on each of you to have your action items completed by the next meeting. If you can't, I'll expect you to inform me in advance."

2. Pair the queen bee with the strongest member of the team and give them a joint assignment. Depend on the other person to make sure the bee does his or her fair share of the work.

3. Whenever you catch the queen bee hiding in the hive or trying to make the worker bees take on his or her responsibilities, call a halt. Gently but firmly, put a stop to the attempt to foist work upon others.

4. Queen bees have become a business buzzword for another reason. Not only are they lazy, they also fail to share information. Their hives are silos and their philosophy is "keep knowledge in and people out." To overcome their

---

The Power of Praise

Few things destroy ambition faster than poorly expressed criticism. And few things take pride out of potential faster than undeserved praise. Listen to your own words. Can you formulate a policy regarding both the positive and negative feedback you give? This one from Charles Schwab, former head of Bethlehem Steel, may help, although you may not wish to go to the extremes he does.

"I consider my ability to arouse enthusiasm among people the greatest asset that I possess, and the way to develop the best that is in people is by appreciation and encouragement. There is nothing else that so kills the ambitions of a person as criticism from his or her superiors. I never criticize anyone. I believe in giving people incentive to work. So I am anxious to praise but loath to find fault. If I like anything, I am hearty in my appreciation and lavish in my praise."

---

tendency to make themselves look good, to defeat their inclination not to help worker bees, try to give collective credit, rather than singling out the efforts of any one person.

If you do choose to isolate people and praise them accordingly, make sure everyone is mentioned at least once during the course of the project.

Power Struggles

Power struggles are a fact of business life—an unpleasant and often ugly fact, but a fact nonetheless. The more loyalty you've built (upwards, downwards, and laterally), the more likely you are to emerge victorious from such struggles. When you've shared your power, then your power range is quite extensive. Consequently, in the struggles that inevitably appear at least once in a career, you're more like to win. Why? Because your opponent will have numerous power-holders with whom to struggle, rather than just one.

Build up your power base—in part by increasing others' obligation to you.

You can also reinforce that base by learning about the various types of power and developing strength in each. There's *charismatic power*, for example, and—despite what you may think—you can actually learn to be charismatic. There's also *position power*, which allows you to exert influence solely on the basis of the role you play.

Additionally, many leaders depend on their *persuasion power* to exert clout for the most positive of outcomes. Think, too, about honing your *expertise power*, which affords you greater control in situations calling for technical knowledge.

Finally, you will occasionally use *reference power*. Use this one carefully so that no one can level charges of favoritism or power abuse against you. *Reference power* or the power of association lets you get some things done more easily by referring to a person or situation that most people respect. If you, for example, are waiting for lab results, you should, and normally would, wait your place in line. But if the president of the company has asked you to obtain those results, you will probably be served more quickly if you refer to his request.

Power and Your Potential as a Leader

Because Lord Acton's quotation provides such a memorable sound bite—"Power tends to corrupt and absolute power corrupts absolutely"—many leaders hesitate to learn the best ways to use power. Consequently, as Harvard's John Kotter remarks, they're failing to optimize their leadership potential.

Don't let this happen to you. Refine your own use of power and help others to benefit from power as well by applying the recommendations in this chapter.

Manager's Checklist for Chapter 7

❏ Develop or maintain a favorable attitude regarding the use of power.

❏ Realize that the more power you give away, the more power you'll actually have.

❏ The greater control your subordinates have over the work they do, the more time you'll have to do leadership tasks.

❏ Empower your team by devising a composite agenda, one they can all buy into.

❑ Force yourself on occasion to move outside your comfort zone and make yourself, your work, your team more visible in the eyes of senior management. Remember that power does not flow to invisible people.

❑ Keep in mind the ethical definition of power: "the judicious use of influence to get things done through other people."

❑ Observe the successful power brokers in your work environment. Learn what they know. Develop your instincts for getting, guarding, giving, and using power well.

❑ Overcome your resistance to the use of power by remembering that indebtedness is really just another way of looking at the old saying, "One hand washes the other."

❑ Use the power of the mind, rather than the power of forcing people. As Napoleon said, the former always wins over the latter.

❑ Don't avoid certain negative associations, such as Machiavellianism, until you've explored the beneficial aspects to be derived from them.

❑ Discuss the five levels (Inform, Investigate, Intend, Initiate, Independent) of empowerment and the levels at which each of your staff members would like to work.

❑ Benefit from the "M-Power" words—mentoring, management, and mindsets.

❑ Use your leadership to make knowledge work in powerful ways, through a skill bank, a corporate notebook, weekly e-mails, a Web site, interviews—to transform information into needed knowledge.

❑ Don't try to avoid organizational politics. Instead, learn to play the political game if you want to move ahead and have your followers move along with you.

❑ Establish a political campaign to win over certain negative types who may be wresting power from you, deliberately or inadvertently, such as the owl, the lamb, the hyena, the lion, and the queen bee.

❏ Use techniques such as Seven's Heaven to invigorate a stalled team and to help ensure all powerful ideas are heard.

❏ Know that power struggles will emerge from time to time. Anticipate them. Prepare yourself and your followers to have ammunition ready, just in case.

❏ Explore the various types of power and make sincere efforts to master each.

The Leader as Liaison

Leadership guru Warren Bennis defines leaders as those who form strategic alliances. His words are echoed by another leadership guru, Stephen Covey: "The future is going to be a time of almost unlimited alliances and partnerships and mergers and acquisitions" (Stephen Covey, *Sky* magazine, p. 87, April 2000). If you're determined to improve your leadership skills and if you're committed to being ready for the future, you need to think of ways to develop or partake of the alliances on which the future will be formed.

You may be thinking your particular organizational role is too small for thinking about alliances. Don't kid yourself. You can make microcosmic alliances, macrocosmic alliances, or numerous alliances in between. You can work as a liaison in effecting partnerships in all kinds of ways. Just blend your creativity with your courage and get going.

Fitting the Pieces Together

An ancient Welsh proverb maintains that the person who would be a leader must also be a bridge. When you serve in a leadership capacity, you in effect serve as a bridge. You bring connection to people and to ideas. You show parallels between the old and the new, the past and the future. You unite entities that might not even have considered combining without your intervention.

Those entities might be individuals, for example, within your own department. In the reflective words of Walt Disney: "Of all the things I've done, the most vital is coordinating those who work with me and aiming their efforts at a certain goal."

But you might also bring cohesion between the current mindset and the new mindset that a given change will require. Broadening your sphere of influence, you might want to form alliances between your department and other departments within the organization or between your team and a focus group of customers. These, of course, are simply examples. The possibilities for you are limited only by the partnerships you can imagine.

Know that partnerships work. Think of the ones you already have in place ... partnerships with staff, with customers (inside or outside the organization), with other managers, other departments, other levels. You've learned that working together works.

Flexibility Rules

There's an old story about two workers that illustrates the need for flexibility in a partnering relationship. One of the men dug a small hole in the ground between the street and the sidewalk. As soon as he finished, his coworker filled it in. Then the two of them moved on to another spot about 10 yards away, where they went through the same procedure. A banker was watching from his desk in the bank across the street. He stared, transfixed. After the fourth repetition, he could take it no longer and went over to inquire about what was going on. "You're making no progress," the productivity-oriented businessman chided.

One of the workmen offered this explanation, "This isn't the way we usually do it. We're supposed to have a third person. After I dig the hole, Jim puts a tree in, and Joe here fills the hole with dirt. But Jim called in sick today." Then he asserted with some pride, "That doesn't mean that Joe and I can't do *our* jobs, though."

Partnering calls for intelligent flexibility. Sometimes, it even calls for one partner to do the work another partner has committed to do.

No matter what the combination is, the intended outcome is always the same: a collaboration that benefits all involved.

Serving as a liaison sometimes means matching the people with questions and the people with answers. It can also mean matching people with a long-range perspective and those able to execute the short-term steps that get us there. In other words, void-identifiers and void-fillers. But such partnering can also pair the strong with the strong in order to build a more capable union. Companies not in competition with each other form strategic unions and frequently even rival companies become allies.

An example of cooperating rivals is the consortium established by the NASA John F. Kennedy Space Center, which has formed an alliance between NASA and eight contractors. The operations analyst who serves as benchmarking coordinator acknowledges that converting closely held trade secrets to collectively used technical expertise may seem like "dancing with the enemy to the uninitiated" (*Quality Care*, Boca Raton: CRC Press, 1998, p. 240). Nonetheless, benefiting from her "chaperoning," the companies involved have developed a model for sharing best practices in a competitive environment. She likens such alliances to power saws that can cut through the organizational barricades imposed by the do-more-with-less era.

Forming Strategic Alliances

As you begin to think about liaising, don't limit yourself to the most immediate sphere in which you have influence. Consider, an ever-widening circle of potential partners—from your immediate workplace, from other parts of your organization, from your industry, perhaps even from your community.

If you keep in mind the truth behind this saying—"The impossible is often the untried"—you'll have no trouble finding a partner. A few possibilities are provided for you here.

Workplace

Partnering is different from teamwork in several ways. Teams usually involve a group of people. While partnering can also involve a group, it could simply be an arrangement between just two people. Teams tend to be permanent work units, whereas partners usually align for a given project. There's also often a difference in terms of mission. The work of teams tends to be mission-critical. The work of partners, by contrast, is work-related but not necessarily mission-related.

Think about the people in your work unit. Whether or not you serve on the same team with them, consider partnering possibilities. For example, you might look at your working relationship with your secretary from a different perspective. In the past, perhaps you basically regarded her as someone in a subordinate position. For the future, consider a partnership arrangement in which your respective opinions regarding the work to be done carry equal merit. Of course, in some matters your opinion would carry more weight, but on many other tasks, her opinion should be regarded quite highly. (Time management experts tell us that a competent secretary can handle 90% of the phone calls coming into the office. In this regard, then, the secretary's role might take precedence over your own.)

Organization

Within the larger organization are uncountable opportunities for partnerships. Finding or being a mentor is but one illustration of how new one-on-one interpersonal arrangements could be formed. Partnering need not include a written agreement. Rather, something as simple as a handshake can cement a relationship that begins with you saying, "I'd like us to look at our working relationship in a different light."

Decide with whom you would most like to improve a working relationship. The list might include internal customers, external ones, suppliers, and certainly people in other departments.

It may help do to a little homework. What other partnerships already exist in the organization? Could you join one of those? Should you? Or is your own challenge so unique that it deserves a unique partnership arrangement? How can you best represent your department as you liaise with another?

Success Through Synergy

Smart Managing In *The Art of Partnering* (Dubuque, IA: Kendall/Hunt Publishing Company, 1994), Ed Rigsbee describes the purpose of the partnering process as the development of synergistic solutions to the challenges faced by each partner. Which of the challenges that you face could best be solved by a partnership?

Industry

With the advance of technology, partners are meeting in cyberspace without ever meeting face to face. If you lack technical skills for getting into cyberspace, someone in your organization has them. Find that person and "partner" with her until you learn how to find industry partners in the electronic world on your own.

You may also find the partner you need for a synergistic solution by attending conferences and trade shows. There, with just a little networking, you can usually find someone knowledgeable about your circumstances and willing to work with you on improving them.

You can even make industry contacts by contacting the author of an article in a trade journal and asking her advice on a challenge you may be facing.

Community

A final, rich source of partnering prospects is the community in which you live. As large as the pool of prospects is, it is often overlooked. Think about all the experts who work at local colleges and universities. Read the yellow pages and remind yourself of the many professionals who live and work in your community. Consider all of the agencies that provide you direct and indirect services.

Next think of issues and concerns you've heard expressed recently. Of all the resources just cited, which would be a good synergistic match with a challenge pressing you or your team?

Here's an illustration. A young woman was mugged one winter evening as she left work and headed to her car in the parking lot. Although she wasn't injured, she was angered at the loss of her handbag. The next morning, she called the local police department and asked if an officer could come to address a group (at no charge) regarding ways women could protect themselves against such incidents. The officer came to the workplace and a great many individuals profited from this ad hoc partnership.

The Prism of Partnership

The prism of partnership has many facets and no two prisms are alike. There is, however, a general set of guidelines that applies to all prisms. They're contained in the six-word rhyme that follows.

Improvise. You've done some creative thinking about sources of partners in the workplace, the organization, the industry, and the community. Likewise, you can improvise or brainstorm some possibilities on your own—from these and other arenas. Be loose and open-ended in your thinking. Improvise as the jazz greats do. (Recall the words of Miles Davis: "Don't do tomorrow what you did yesterday.")

Advise. Once you've selected a potential partner and contacted her, engage in an informal discussion. This is the time to advise her of your intentions. Honestly specify what you're willing to give and what you'd like to get in return.

Devise. Based on the information that emerged in the Advise stage, you'll next work out an agreement that details, basically, who will do what by when.

Supervise. Few things move along on their own momentum. Most need a push or prod from an active partner. When you supervise in a partnership, you monitor. You check in. You check on. You even check up to ensure things are going in the direction both parties wanted. Your partner, naturally, will do the same from time to time.

Surprise. The best partnerships work because there's been a show of mutual respect. One way to demonstrate your appreciation for a partnership that works is to surprise your partner

Hesitant?

Smart Managing Quotations often serve to embolden us when we're hesitant or doubtful. If you're reluctant to start a partnership, think about this comment from author Carlos Castaneda, "We either make ourselves miserable or we make ourselves strong. The amount of work is the same." Instead of groaning and moaning about a situation you wish were better, do something. Form an alliance and watch improvement happen from the combined strengths.

on occasion with a card, a single flower, a handwritten note, etc. Such unexpected gestures are known as *lagniappes*; they go a long way toward building trust and respect.

Revise. During the course of your partnership arrangement, think of ways to revise the original agreement to make it work better for you. And, when the purpose has been fulfilled, take time to evaluate the success of the collaboration. Ask yourself, "If I had to do it over again, what would I revise?" Your answers will help you design future partnerships that come even closer to the targets you establish.

The Six C's of Partnering

In addition to the verbs we've just looked at, partnership agreements are usually characterized by their attention to the following nouns.

Commitment. If the partner you approach seems halfhearted about the arrangement, avoid entering into it. In fact, you should preface your overture with a gracious exit. A line like this works smoothly: "Sue, I'd like to propose something to you but—before I do—I want you to feel absolutely comfortable telling me if you're not interested or if you don't have time. I promise I won't be offended. In fact, if you participate without being fully committed, it would make it very difficult for me. So, please, be totally honest with me. It'll be better for both of us if you are."

Partnerships work only if the partners do. It'll be hard for you to uphold your half of the bargain if your partner has already abandoned hers.

Communications. Determine early on the preference each of you has for the type and frequency of communications. Also iron out the calendar voids: When will you be on vacation and thus unreachable? When are your weekly staff meetings held? These small details will facilitate subsequent exchanges. And, when you do connect, try to keep your messages friendly but short, professional but specific.

Creativity. A glance at any major newspaper on any given day will show how extensive partnering is. From some of these collaborations you'll derive ideas for ways to improve your own work processes and productivity. When a copy company turns to a catalog company to learn how to fill orders more quickly, it shows the transferability of processes across industries.

You, too, can profit from cross-industry practices. Who stands out in your mind as a leader in some aspect of manufacturing, service, or hospitality? Using one such exemplar, what could you hope to learn and then apply to your own business practices?

Questions like these are but one creative way to locate prospects.

Another is to juxtapose two or three completely unrelated words and see what partnership ideas emerge as a result of this verbal union. (The technique works for a myriad of other situations, too.) Assume you want to improve your training program and you want a creative approach to partnering. Here's how you do it. Throw three words together, such as *hedge, music,* and *lamp.* What ideas come to mind as you study these words in combination?

"Hedge" might make you think of the phrase "hedging your bets" and that might lead to thoughts of gambling. Consequently, you might be led to a partner who works in the legalized gambling industry. She could be part of the state lottery system or an

Indian reservation casino or even an employee from the Atlantic City or Las Vegas resorts. Through her, you might obtain some ideas about how to attract customers to programs.

"Music" could inspire you to include music in some of your programs. So, if you were doing a class on team building, you might partner with a nearby school for a short chamber-music concert to illustrate the need for everyone to "read from the same sheet of music."

The "lamp" word could make you think of a company you believe is "enlightened" on training. At the very least, you could establish a telephone partnership with someone in the training department of that firm. Do some informal benchmarking. Learn both the "how's" and "what's" that constitute their approach to training.

Culture. What one word would you use to describe the culture in which you spend so much of every working day? Is it a culture of "accomplishment"? A culture of "respect"? A culture of "creativity"? A culture of "partnership"? If the last label is not the one you'd apply to your surroundings, then you have some work to do.

Begin by building awareness of the benefits of partnering. Talk about it in staff meetings.

Send out periodic memos on the topic. Plan to hold a drawing each month for those who are partnering. (You may want to partner with local merchants for some of the prizes.)

Climbing Ivy
TOOLS Ivy Lee is the management consultant credited with making productivity climb by 30% at Bethlehem Steel. He did it with a simple list: "Things to do today." Your efforts to improve the culture need not be costly in terms of time, money, or effort. But they do need to be consistent, pervasive, and persuasive.

After you've built awareness, it's time to build partnerships. While you're improvising, advising, devising, supervising, surprising, and revising with your partner, you're simultaneously modeling the behavior you want others to adopt. When leaders in a particular culture exemplify the behaviors they applaud, it's so much easier for others to follow their lead.

Conflict. You're old enough to know it's not a perfect world. And, despite best intentions, things do go wrong in partnerships. Anticipate conflicts, disagreements, and flareups. Work out a solution plan before the problems erupt. The plan might include one or more of the following mediation techniques. (Many others are possible as well.)

- If the two parties reach a stalemate, a third, neutral person will be brought in to break the tie vote. Both partners will identify and agree to this person at the onset of the partnership agreement.
- If the partnership involves three or more parties, a simple majority-rules vote will decide issues.
- If any one of the parties involves is unable or unwilling to continue the partnership, she needs to simply terminate the agreement with a verbal announcement.
- For decisions both parties feel are major and on which they're unable to agree, two managers (one selected by each party) will be given the details and asked to recommend a decision.

Commonality. When you form a liaison with another person, group, or institution, you operate on the belief that you have something in common. Generally speaking, this commonality is the shared desire to benefit from each other's expertise. Specifically, though, you must have several other commonalities on which your alliance is based.

It helps if your values are shared values and your purpose one to which you'll both adhere. Talk about such things with your partner before you cement the relationship. Learn how realistic the proposed partnership is and if you can both commit to the timeframe it'll require. Ensure that necessary approvals are in place before either of you invests much time or effort. Will you both derive benefit from this arrangement? If lopsided results will occur, one side or the other will be less inclined to participate.

When you liaise, especially in your initial overtures, learn as much as you can about the other party in regard to your mutual interest. And share as much as you can so that commonalities can be determined and differences disregarded.

Listening

The positive effect good listening can have on followers is perhaps best shown in the story of a society matron in Great Britain. She was so prominent a figure in London society that she managed to have dinner with Prime Minister William Gladstone and then with his political rival, Benjamin Disraeli.

Asked what she thought of these two distinguished statesmen, she revealed a key truth about communication. "When I left the dining room after sitting next to Mr. Gladstone, I thought he was the cleverest man in England." Quite a tribute for the prime minister. Her next words, however, paid even greater homage to the listening skills possessed by Disraeli. "After sitting next to Mr. Disraeli, though, I thought *I* was the cleverest *woman* in England.

Of course, your audiences are typically more professional than dinner guests. Nonetheless, you'll find success comes to you more easily, no matter who you're dealing with, if you can listen well. Listen to what is being said and to what is *not* being said. Listen to people and nature and trends and statistics. Listen to the grapevine or visit the rumor mill on occasion. Listen to insiders and outsiders alike.

Your decision about whom to partner with on what facet of business should be subject to a number of influences, both animate and inanimate.

The Listening Log Given the lightning-bolt rapidity with which information is sent to us on an hourly basis, it's often difficult to recall details, even important details. We recommend you get in the habit or recording insights or interesting tidbits at least once a day. These are not management facts or stats but rather peripheral threads that can be woven at a later time into the fabric of partnering.

Your decisions about partnering—or about many other aspects of your work—should not be based on static patterns. Rather, they should reflect the dynamic nature of a growing, ever-changing force. This force emerges from conflicting currents, many moving in opposite directions, in the social/ emotional/psychological/ intellectual context of the work environment.

The Trust Factor

To avoid being swept away by these fast-moving currents, you have to build a trust strong enough to withstand power shifts. Whether you're partnering, managing, or leading, you should have long ago given up the Taylor model. Based on the principles of Frederick Taylor, this model depends on precisely defined jobs and the behaviors that get those jobs done. Such precision leaves little room for workers to think or act independently. Of that model, Konosuke Matsushita, Executive Advisor of the electric company that bears his name, had this to say in an address to Western industrialists in 1979: "Your firms are built on the Taylor model, where your bosses do the thinking while your workers wield the screwdrivers."

In an empowered workplace, leaders trust their followers to do more than manual labor. By extension, the more you respect both the manual and mental talents of your followers, the more likely you are to find and optimize partnering opportunities.

To develop trust around partnering issues with your staff, ask for brainstormed suggestions about people and organizations with whom you and your team can partner. Record and then study the ideas. Once you've made your decision, make certain to let your team know it was the result of their input. Thank them accordingly.

Such actions reflect your character. They show you're not just mouthing the right words but that you're *meaning* the right words.

You have to reflect that same character as you develop trust with your partners. In the most obvious way, you do this by giving your word and not taking it back. When your partner real-

> **⚠️ CAUTION!**
> ## Trust Me!
>
> A note of caution is warranted here. Yes, it's important to trust and to build trust. But there's a fine line you have to walk. If you trust too much, others might take advantage of you. The results could negatively impact not only you but your organization as well. Be mindful of author Frank Crane's observation, "You may be deceived if you trust too much, but you will live in torment if you do not trust enough."
>
> Protect yourself and the partnership by anticipating certain pitfalls and making accommodations for them in advance. Find your own balance between trusting too much and not trusting enough.

---

izes that you'll keep your word or provide an honest explanation of why you cannot, you've gone a long way toward the honor that exists among thieves and partners alike.

When you and your partner have mutual trust, you do more than keep your word. When those words become angry, you trust each other enough to explore the causes rather than simply end the partnership. There is a shared faith that the partnership is more important than the occasional flareup. Even if you have to return to the divisive issue at a later time, you'll do that, because the sum you've created together is greater than the individual parts.

A Word to the Wise

Your job description probably does *not* contain the requirement to liaise. Nonetheless, as a leader intent on effecting positive change, you're no doubt determined to find creative ways to reach out to others and to formulate new plans, policies, procedures, projects, and processes on the basis of what you can do together. Some courage is required for the leader as liaison. But that won't surprise *you*, for you know that "coward" and "leader" are antonyms, not synonyms!

Manager's Checklist for Chapter 8

❏ Think globally and act locally in making liaisons. You can even act globally: great plans have power to stir the soul.

❏ Go outside the boundaries of your job description to explore connections that have never existed before. Leaders are bridges; they pass over boundaries to unite related and unrelated entities in new ways. Managers, by contrast, typically stay inside established boundaries.

❏ Fill existing voids.

❏ Liaise with competitors, to fill both common needs and different needs. Keep your manager apprised, though, to avoid charges of "sleeping with the enemy."

❏ Regard your professional circumstances as a jigsaw puzzle. When you think about partners, look beyond your workplace, to the organization, to the industry, and to the various parts of the larger community.

❏ Spend time on all six of these rhyming words as you proceed through the partnership's life cycle: Improvise, Advise, Devise, Supervise, Surprise, and Revise.

❏ Attend to the six C's of effective liaison relationships: Get Commitment all the way around. Establish clear Communications. Demonstrate Creativity in finding synergistic solutions. Develop a Culture in which strategic alliances can flourish. Anticipate Conflict and have a strategy be ready for resolving it. Determine the Commonalities that connect you to your partner and reinforce the values you both share—before, during, and after the liaison.

❏ Listen to the many influences that can help you decide with whom to form liaisons and can help make the alliance more successful. And don't expect to find the "voices" you need to hear in the usual places.

❏ Trust, but don't trust everyone, all the time, in all circumstances. Build trust by doing what you say you'll do and valuing your followers and your partners.

The Leader as Planner

Managers deal with the cut and dried, the straight and narrow, the hard and fast rules and regulations. Leaders, by contrast, often venture forth into the unknown. They make the rules, rather than abide by them.

This adventurous spirit is especially important for the leader as planner. That's because of the tendency of best-laid plans to go astray. When they do, leaders have to be flexible. They must adjust to new circumstances quickly. They need to feel exhilaration rather than discouragement by unexpected turns of events.

In large measure, leaders understand the futility of planning for the future. But they also understand the need to have charted a course, even though turbulence might throw them off it. Events that result in drastic change are often such remote possibilities that they're not even planned for. For example, the Oklahoma City bombing was a tragedy no one saw coming. Ideally, we'll never know such horror again. But now we'll be more prepared should such terrorism occur.

Similarly, epidemics like AIDS were not foreseen, nor were attacks of killer bees or flesh-eating organisms. The potential for breakup of Microsoft was a possibility its founders probably never considered. But anticipating the unanticipated has become an industry unto itself. There are magazines and conferences entirely devoted to planning for contingencies that will probably never occur but that require us to be ready, just in case.

In this chapter we'll discuss various types of plans, the myths surrounding them, and tools and recommendations for maximizing their usefulness.

Long-Range Plans

On the individual level, you've learned that success is really a question of putting the "I should's" ahead of the "I want's." You learned long ago to envision the future you wanted for yourself and perhaps even for your family. You committed to certain sacrifices in order to turn the vision into reality. Whatever the vision is, it can be equated with the long-range planning an organization conducts in order to achieve its own vision.

You've learned to postpone gratification, sleep, and self-indulgence in order to get a degree, a promotion, or a raise. Similarly, if the corporation is intent on expanding into new markets, new countries, or new lines of production; if it's determined to reduce costs or reorganize or build customer loyalty—it knows certain changes will have to be made.

Leaders know that breakthroughs typically come about as the result of a *kaizen* approach. Gradual, incremental milestones are achieved on the road to ultimate victory.

The benefits associated with planning apply to all kinds of plans. They include savings of time, money, and effort; better coordination and control; facility in delegating; reduction or elimination of wasteful steps; and improved morale through controlling chaos, to some extent at least.

> **Kaizen** A process of making continuous improvement on a regular basis. Masaaki Imai, in his groundbreaking book *Kaizen* (New York: McGraw-Hill, 1986), introduced Americans to this concept, which has long worked in Japan. In time, the small achievements lead to the big success.

Your long-term or strategic plans ideally begin with a strategic vision, a vision that inspires others. But even if you don't have a vision in mind, you can delineate one after careful attention to questions like the following.

- What are the most critical issues facing us today?
- What forces are shaping the critical issues for tomorrow?
- What do technology experts have to say about advances in the next decade?
- What do we as an organization do and do well right now?
- What do we do but not so well?
- What will our customers want from us in the years ahead?
- Where will the most substantial profit centers be?
- What opportunities are we missing?
- What big mistakes have we and others in our industry made in the last five years?
- What relevance does the following quote from management expert Warren Bennis have for us? "The factory of the future will have only two employees, a man and a dog. The man will be there to feed the dog. The dog will be there to keep the man from touching the equipment."

No matter how large or small your role as leader, no matter the scope of the leadership efforts you've undertaken, you still need a sense of what the enhanced future will look like. Change for the sake of change is worthless. Change that effects improvement on existing conditions is the only change worth undergoing. So, as you seek to change things, as opposed to maintaining the status quo, what vision guides you? What will be better?

Once you have clarity surrounding the new status you'll be creating, then you can work backwards in a sense to figure out what the mission will be and what smaller goals and objectives you'll need to support that mission.

If your style is democratic or participative, you'll want to invite your followers to help shape the vision. If you tend to be more autocratic, you may have a singular vision that you use to

> ## Planned Evolution
> CAUTION!
>
> "The only things that evolve by themselves in an organization are disorder, friction, and malperformance." Given the fact that the author of these words, Peter Drucker, is honored around the world for his management wisdom, few of us would dare disagree. Let's assume Drucker is correct. Then, you have a strong impetus for planning here in order to avoid chaos, conflict, and lackluster performance. Your vision will be the ideal, your mission will indicate the real path to that ideality, and your goals will become the practical translation of the mission.

inspire others to accomplishment. And if you have the classic laissez-faire approach, you might find followers coming to you with their vision and having you champion it. All three approaches will work. What really matters is the worth of the vision and the extent to which it is fought for.

Medium-Range Plans

Medium-range plans answer the question, "What do we need to do to make the vision a reality?" The mission that results becomes the driving force behind the concerted efforts of your team. As you begin to make decisions that will move the vision from the darkness of the unknown to the light of implementation, use both the worm's eye and the bird's eye view.

The worm's eye perspective is more detailed, more literal, more "down-to-earth," if you will. While it lacks the grandeur of the big picture the bird can see, the worm's view nonetheless provides value. If you think about the bird and the worm in a forest, then you can look at mission and vision like this: the mission keeps the team grounded by focusing on the trees that constitute the metaphoric forest of the vision. By nurturing those trees, the leader and his team ensure the forest is kept alive.

In thinking about the elements that constitute mission success, consider:

- customers
- the workforce
- markets

- technology
- world events
- innovation

Each of these, and other elements, can and should play an important role in helping you fashion a mission statement that basically tells supporters what must be done to reach the vision via the mission.

Let's look at a vision statement from a security company: "To run a profitable, first-class operation dedicated to client safety and security." It's lofty, it's idealistic, it soars to the realm of the nearly unattainable.

Now look at the mission statement that derives from the vision: "To hire quality personnel; to use up-to-date technology; to innovate based on needs of current and future customers." The mission suggests three areas the leader and his team can pursue in order to make the vision a reality: hiring practices, technology, and customer relations. Hiring the best-qualified staff will help move the company into the realm of first-class operations. So, too, will using the most modern and effective technology. The ideal of profitability is indirectly addressed in the phrase

Analyze Forces in the Field

TOOLS Psychologist Kurt Lewin is credited with devising a simple tool, force field analysis, that helps planners obtain a wide-angle view on a problem. Essentially, the planning team begins by stating the vision or ideal state at the top of a sheet of paper. Beneath it, the current state is written. As an example, the ideal might be zero defects. The current error rate might be seven percent. Then the paper is divided into two columns. On the left are written the driving forces, those aspects of the work environment that could lead to error-free work. On the right are listed those forces that might prevent or that do prevent employees from performing such work. Once ideas have been generated, the team decides what is the best course of action to pursue in order to achieve the standard of six-sigma or nearly perfect production.

The mission statement that evolves might specify forming teams to help each worker produce the highest-caliber product. From this, goals are specified covering team formation, training, etc.

"future customers." But both current customers and those who will come from increased marketing efforts will be encouraged to express their needs. From those needs, the company will make appropriate adjustments and innovations.

Short-Term Plans

Strategic planning begins with a vision, which is then translated to a mission. To carry out the mission, short-term goals or operational plans are required. The primary goal is broken down into smaller goals, through the following steps.

- Define the objective behind a given goal.
- Make a list of all the tasks required in order to achieve this goal.
- Assign the appropriate people to carry out the tasks.
- Evaluate the effectiveness of executed tasks.
- Make adjustments accordingly.
- Revise a former objective or formulate a new one.

Considering the security company we looked at earlier, the phrase that spoke to customer satisfaction—"to innovate based on the needs of current and future customers"—can now be broken down into short-term goals, such as forming a focus group, for example.

Shattering the Myths

A great many myths surround the topic of leadership in general and planning in particular. Let's examine some of the most common.

Myth 1: Plans Stifle Creativity

You probably know some people who have all the ingredients necessary for success but just can't seem to find the right recipe. They squander their talents because they have trouble finding a course of action to pursue. Planning is the recipe you need. Yes, you may be the sort of cook who likes to experiment and do your own thing. And perhaps you've been successful with this "winging it" approach.

TRICKS OF THE TRADE

Say It Again, Sam

One technique that promotes creativity and clarity at the same time requires you as leader to state what your plan is—long-term, medium-term, or even short-term. The second person on the team will restate what he thinks you've said, without repeating any of the actual words you used. An observer notes any discrepancies and jots them down. The third person gives his understanding of the plan, without using the key terms that you or the second person employed. Again, the observer records the ways in which the definition is expanding, shrinking, or otherwise changing.

After each person has had a chance to give his interpretation, the observer shares his notes and a discussion follows. In this way, you can help ensure everyone is reading from the same sheet of music.

Others, however, both above you and below you in the organizational structure, will want to see a plan. They'll expect your vision to be clearly defined, your mission to be clearly articulated, and your goals to be as familiar to them as they are to you. You may have to put your natural "play it by ear" tendencies aside when you serve as leader. Your followers deserve much more. And yes, you can still be creative even though you've made detailed plans.

It's a myth that people can't be creative when they plan.

Myth 2: Not Reaching a Goal Equals Failure

Another myth is that if you don't reach your goal, you've failed. On the contrary, not reaching your goal sometimes turns out to be the best thing that can happen. This situation is akin to the old warning: "Be careful what you wish for because your wishes might come true." If the goal was the wrong goal, or if you had the wrong people trying to reach it, or if a better goal came along, so to speak, then you'll celebrate not reaching the first goal.

Benjamin Eliah Mays, former president of Morehouse College, once said, "The tragedy in life does not lie in not reaching your goal. The tragedy lies in having no goal to reach. It is not a disaster not to be able to capture your ideal, but it is a disaster to have no ideal to capture. It is not a disgrace not to reach the stars, but it is a disgrace to have no stars to reach for. It is not failure, but low aim that is a sin."

Myth 3: Plans Represent Unrealistic Dreams

It's true that plans have been called "dreams with deadlines." But that doesn't mean they're unreachable. The next time you're tempted to put off planning because you think it's a pie-in-the-sky exercise in futility, think about John Goddard. At the age of 15, Goddard set himself 127 challenging lifetime goals. Among them was the wish to lead the first expedition to explore the length of the Nile, the world's longest river (4,160 miles). He did this. He also sought to explore the second longest river in the world. He also did this—the 2,700-mile Congo River in Zaire (now the Democratic Republic of the Congo). His adventures include setting records as a civilian jet flier and an altitude record of 63,000 feet in the F-106. Goddard has achieved well over 100 of his goals.

Make your plans achievable. But also make them challenging enough so spirits can soar.

Myth 4: Challenging Goals Cause Undue Stress

In fact, the opposite is true. Challenging goals have a way of galvanizing a team. The excitement of having BHAGs (Big, Hairy, Audacious Goals—a term coined by author Jim Collins) energizes followers who find a renewed confidence in themselves and their collective efforts. Difficult goals usually result in higher performance than easy goals do.

Planning Tools

Talk to those around you who are good planners. Learn what tools they use. The more tools in your planning tool kit, the more easily you can make plans that work. Here are two of the most popular tools—the flow chart and the evaluation matrix.

Flowchart

The flowchart is one of the most popular tools for planners. It graphically represents the steps in a given process and uses a mere four symbols to indicate the sequence of activities.

An *oval* is used to show where the process starts and where the process ends. Determine what input gets the process going—that's your starting point. When the output has been created, that particular process is over. In between are *rectangles*, which are the actual steps in the process. *Arrows* are used to connect the steps. When you reach a decision point, a question answerable by "yes" or "no," then you use the *diamond* shape. If yes, continue; if no, you take an alternative step (see Figure 9-1).

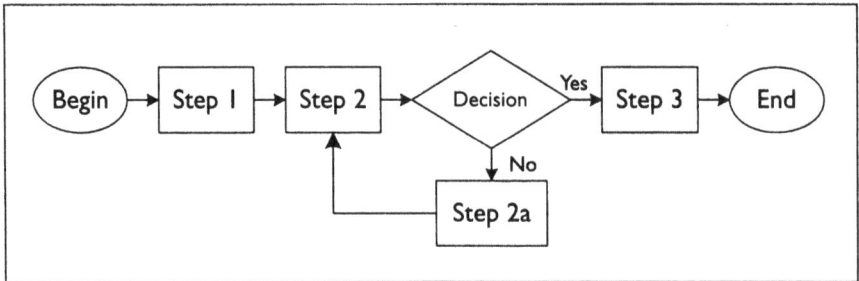

Figure 9-1. What a flowchart looks like

In addition to showing the process as it actually works—and you can flowchart a small process or the overall system—you can do a second flow diagram showing how the process or system would work ideally. By comparing the two, you'll find out where waste, duplication, and unnecessary steps are occurring.

The flowchart tells how specific processes or larger systems can be improved. Once ideas have been generated, the evaluation matrix will help you decide the most viable of options.

Evaluation Matrix

This is another simple tool that allows planners to choose among alternatives. Time is limited, after all, and teams cannot pursue every possibility they think of to achieve their goals. Once a list of alternatives has been generated, you and your team establish criteria—important aspects to be considered for the plan of action that will lead to the goals.

For example, if you were buying a new copier for the office and had listed six possible models as your alternatives, you might list certain features or cost limits as your criteria. Three or four should suffice.

> **Toxins in the Bloodstream of Idealism**
> Words without the actions to back them up have been
> defined as the "assassins of idealism" by former presi-
> dent Herbert Hoover. Plans are more than black marks on white
> paper. They are the road maps that take people where they both need
> and want to go. As the team's tour guide, in a matter of speaking, you
> have a responsibility to keep plans living, working documents. Post
> them as prominently and publicly as you can. And show the periodic
> progress being made on those plans.

Then rate each alternative in terms of how well it meets
each of the criteria. You can use simple terms such as "poor,"
"average," and "excellent." Each person then votes on the rank-
ing he would give each alternative. Their votes are recorded.
The alternative(s) with the highest vote becomes the course of
action for the team to pursue.

Things to Remember

Managers and leaders both don and doff a great many hats in
the course of a given work week. But the planning hat is one of
the most exciting of all to wear. It represents the opportunity to
bring good ideas to life. There are certain provisos to bear in
mind, of course. Several are explored in the section that follows.

Janitors, Soldiers, and Statesmen

You've probably heard the story about the metropolitan muse-
um that was planning to hire a consultant to determine which of
its numerous exhibits drew the largest crowds. On the basis of
that information, they could plan for future exhibits that would
draw the most museum-goers *and* the most in entrance fees.
Just prior to voting on the budget for the study, one of the com-
mittee members had a really bright idea. "Why not just ask the
janitor," he proposed, "where he has to mop the hardest?"

Ivan Seidenberg, chairman and CEO of Bell Atlantic
Corporation, makes it a practice to ask various employees for
information and advice (Daniel Levine, "My First Job," *Reader's
Digest*, January 1997, p. 90). He admits his practice stems

from a janitor experience as well. When he was a very young man and working his way through school, he had a conversation one day with a janitor who told him that some firms will pay for their employees to go to college. He cited utility companies in particular. Seidenberg went to work for a phone company immediately and has worked in no other field since.

As we've learned from the quality movement, people closest to the process are frequently the most knowledgeable about it. As you plan, don't make the mistake of thinking only managers have the requisite vision for formulating the direction in which progress should be made. Involve people from all levels of the organization (and even some outside the organization) so 360-degree planning can occur.

In addition to the Seidenberg advice, consider the Clausewitz caveat. Karl von Clausewitz was a Prussian military strategist who is probably more famous for the following observation than for his many exploits on the battlefield: "Beware the brilliance of transient events." Determining which events are transient and which will have profound effects upon the organizational future is difficult. The title of "leader," after all, does not confer omniscience. Others will understand if you're occasionally blinded by brilliance.

Perhaps the best you can do is give brilliant events careful thought. Then, working in concert with others, determine if those events truly have the impact they seemed to have at first.

Remember the Machiavellian observation: "In the beginning, problems are easy to cure but hard to diagnose; with the passage of time, having gone unrecognized and unattended, they become easy to diagnose but hard to cure." When planning, act on the information you have, react to the information that comes in, but "pro-act," too: look for resolutions of problems that have not yet been identified.

To refine your planning skills, read a biography or biographical sketch of figures whose plans have had tremendous impact upon the way we work and live. Record their viewpoints and their secrets and refer to your notes at least once a month, preferably before leading a planning session.

Intuition

Some planners have such faith in their intuitive powers that they rely more on hunches than on data. There's nothing wrong with this approach *if* you're certain your intuition works.

One way to determine if it does is to keep a log for a whole month of decisions made by intuition and decisions made by planning and relying on input. If your intuition-based decisions yield results as positive as your data-based decisions, then continue intuiting. Formulate plans based on what you "feel" is the direction to go in.

However, if your results are less than stellar, you may want to rethink your basic style of planning and subsequent decision-making. Take this simple test to discover how intuitive you really are. Circle the letter you think has the best definition for each word.

> ### Use Bacon to Avoid Egg on Your Face
>
> Hundreds of years ago, Francis Bacon asserted that "man prefers to believe that which he prefers to be true." It's tempting to base plans on what you know is true and what you want to be true. Such plans, however, tend to come back and bite you in areas better reserved for sitting. To avoid a shaky foundation for long-range, medium-range, and short-range plans, ask tough questions, benchmark, and gather input from the least likely of sources, including those with whom you're not on the best of terms.

1. "Quidnunc" means
   a. an instrument used by photographers to determine light intensity
   b. to hunt for airborne butterflies
   c. a person who gossips
   d. the name of a special glue used on envelopes

2. "Firn" means
   a. granular snow at the top of a glacier
   b. an abnormal passage from an abscess to the skin
   c. a fragile leaf stem
   d. a shelter for poultry

3. "Ichthyosis" means
   a. a meteor that radiates from a constellation
   b. a respiratory illness
   c. a congenital skin disease
   d. a doctrine of moral perfection

4. "Phut" means
   a. a term for a wasting disease such as tuberculosis
   b. a group of synthetic dyes
   c. restricted to a small area or scope
   d. a dull, flat sound

5. "Sublate" means
   a. a religious article of clothing
   b. to contradict or deny
   c. the part of oil that does not become solid
   d. the coat of arms of a French royal family

Once you've marked your intuitive choices, you can check the power of your intuition by turning to the end of the chapter. If you had three or more correct, you probably *do* have some powers of intuition. We still recommend, though, keeping a log to ascertain the value of your intuitively based plans.

In addition to remembering not to use intuition exclusively, keep in mind that self-confidence can actually work against you if it prevents you from studying a situation in depth. If you're the type who has experienced success in the past, you may be tempted to let that experience circumvent research necessary for effective planning. Other pitfalls are described as follows.

Pitfalls

Why don't people plan more and/or better? There are almost as many reasons why plans fail as there are types of management styles. In part, we don't plan or plan well because we have a tendency to "wing it," to "shoot from the hip," to struggle against boundaries and confinements. We Americans cherish spontaneity and freedom and independence of thought and action. To many, plans are simply too restrictive; they are regarded as creativity-crushers.

Stratification

Intuiting is different from detecting emerging patterns.
Stratification is a tool that will help you see beginning trends.
Take a workplace problem and brainstorm with your team the possible causes of that situation. Try for a list of 30 items. Then, stratify by clustering each of the items in one of five or six broad categories. Study the categories or stratifications to learn what may be the root cause of the problem. Often, it's related to a stratification we hadn't even considered.

This attitude is only one of many barriers to effective planning. Which of these additional reasons have you used to explain why your own planning is/was not as effective as it could be?

- Not enough time
- Not enough data provided in advance of the planning session
- People who should have participated in the planning did not
- Couldn't get approval for plans
- Reluctance to try anything new
- Belief that planning is futile, given the unpredictability of business today
- Office politics
- Waited too long to set up the plans
- Failed to get buy-in for the plan
- Too many agendas, hidden and open
- Poor definition of the problem
- Don't know how to plan

Planning is not for the fainthearted, for it requires considerable time and effort. However, without plans, you'll probably not achieve the success of which you and your followers are capable. Use the tools, tips, and techniques in this chapter to help refine your long-, medium-, and short-range planning.

Planning reflects an intellectual orderliness. It suggests to those around you that you care enough about the project to invest time and thought to effect the best possible outcomes. Planning also makes it easier for your followers to execute the vision you believe in.

Manager's Checklist for Chapter 9

❏ Anticipate the unanticipated and perhaps even the unanticipatable.

❏ Make long-range plans that sustain your vision.

❏ Don't expect immediate breakthroughs. Plan for *kaizen* or small, incremental improvements.

❏ Cite the benefits of planning to your planning team.

❏ Ask numerous questions to help refine your plans.

❏ Don't plan changes just for the sake of change. Make certain the changes will result in improved circumstances.

❏ Remember the words of Peter Drucker—the only things that evolve by themselves are negative things. The positive things you have to plan for.

❏ Use whatever leadership style you're comfortable with when you plan. The value lies in the plans, not in the style.

❏ Medium-range plans and mission go together. If the vision is the painting, the mission is the broad brush strokes and the goal is the fine brush strokes.

❏ Don't use singular inputs for planning. Turn to many sources and resources.

❏ Employ tools like the force field analysis to gain a full understanding of the situation you are seeking to improve.

❏ Follow these steps when doing short-term planning. Define the objective, list the tasks, match people to tasks, evaluate progress, and make adjustments as needed. Once you've determined the effectiveness of the adjustments, continue with the plan, calibrate it once again, or perhaps abandon it and devise another.

❏ Don't let myths about planning limit your success. Plans

do not stifle creativity, they don't have to be unrealistic, they don't have to cause stress. And, if you don't hit your intended target, you don't have to think of failure. You still will have learned, gained, and grown on the way.

❏ Use flow charts and evaluation matrixes as planning tools.

❏ Post your plans and show the progress being made with them.

❏ Remember what we learned from the janitor (talk to many people as you plan), the soldier (beware the brilliance of transient events), and the statesman (diagnose and treat problems early).

❏ Be careful about believing what you prefer to be true. Obtain opposing viewpoints whenever you can.

❏ Rely on your intuition only if you're certain you can.

❏ Stratify to spot emerging trends.

❏ Don't make the planning pitfalls excuses. Vow to overcome them before they upset your plans.

Answers to the intuitive quiz: 1. c; 2. a; 3. c; 4. d; 5. b

The Leader as . . . Leader

Above all else, the leader is a person who exemplifies the trait Theodore Roosevelt regarded as the single most important ingredient in the formula of success: "knowing how to get along with people." Leaders demonstrate adaptability. They can accommodate themselves to different kinds of people, different projects, different places, different positions. The concept of leader as a person who facilitates the success of all is an accurate one and throughout this book, we've attempted to convey the importance of the leader as a person playing many roles.

A brief recap of those positions follows.

The Leader Defined

To be sure, leaders and managers share a number of traits. Among them are a positive attitude toward the organization, the team, the work. Both managers and leaders generally have positive attitudes, although the leader's tends to be more action-oriented than the manager's. When you have on your manager's hat, you're wading in familiar waters; you're doing an outstanding job of the duties specified in your job description. By contrast,

154

when you're wearing the leader's hat, you may be stepping into unknown waters, the swirling eddies of which may make you vulnerable. This is the basic difference in the two roles. No matter which hat you're wearing, though, you demonstrate honesty, fairness, trustworthiness, and respect if you wish to be called outstanding.

You both manage and lead by example and promote diversity of thought, action, and staff. You work to meet customer requirements and work collaboratively with those inside and outside the organization. Whether you're managing or leading, you have opportunities to coach, to motivate and challenge employees, to encourage growth. Part of your many-faceted job includes removing barriers to others' productivity.

In both roles, you're expected to have sound judgment, to accept responsibility, to support those who have joined you in making decisions. Your competence is assumed and others expect you to perform your job according to the highest possibly standards. You're also expected to make continuous improvements in that job, although as a leader, you'll be more willing to incur risk as you do.

Leaders apply the concept of continuous improvement to themselves and their followers as well as to processes. They acquire old knowledge, create new knowledge, and share both with those who need to know. Leaders are also inclined to think outside the box and to find novel solutions for problems. They are typically systems thinkers who aim for big-picture thinking that results in "wins" for many stakeholders.

As we've noted, you demonstrate certain actions regardless of the role you're playing. For example, you need to recognize and reward your team whenever they've met a milestone or reached a goal. And you put the organization's needs above your own and work to serve a larger audience than "self."

The Leader as Visionary

That attention to issues bigger than your own is seen in another definition. Joseph Jaworski, attorney-turned-author

(*Synchronicity: The Inner Path of Leadership*, San Francisco: Berrett-Koehler, 1996), asserts that the leader's job is successful discovery of the organization's destiny and the courage to follow that destiny. When you serve as visionary, you may be discovering a destiny others have established or you may actually be creating that destiny. Without it, though, it'll be very difficult for you to lead others.

A fascinating insight into the courage required of people in leadership roles can be found in ancient maps. The lands that had never been explored were designated as "terra incognita," "there be dragons," and sometimes the alluring phrase "more beyond." If you can envision what lies beyond the known, if you've been known to take on an organizational dragon or two, then you probably have the stuff of which leaders are made.

That "stuff" includes an awareness of external forces, some of which whisper what the future holds. Those whispers are clues. They hint at what will be and what will be important. But the leader blinded by her own agenda will not hear the whispers or see the clues. Such leaders aren't learning lessons. They're not reinventing. They're not, quite simply, attuned to emerging needs.

The Leader as Problem-Solver

Synonymous with both management and leadership is the need to solve problems. Operating always from an ethical stance, the leaders we applaud often embrace the difficulties inherent in problems and are exhilarated by the opportunity to convert crisis to calm. Leaders cause change with their solutions and don't apologize for doing so.

Does your attitude match that of the man who solved a very big automotive problem? "It's the job of leaders to set the rules and enforce the rules and, most important, when the rules don't work any more, to change the rules," Lee Iacocca insisted. Do you have the courage of a Lee Iacocca when you face problems?

Naturally, you need more than courage to stand out as a leader who solves problems effectively. You also need a willingness to view a given situation from an atypical perspective.

Look at this example and you'll see what we mean. Imagine you heard about a man who finally got out of jail. The first thing he did was push a car to a nearby hotel. Then he left a large amount of money there. His next action was similar: he pushed the car to a house in the area and left money there, too, although less money than he'd left at the hotel.

What explanation can you give for this scenario?

Another example requires you to study these letters and "translate" them into a familiar phrase:

Ph.D.

M.D.

Ed.D.

0

If your thinking was divergent, you'd have recognized progression on a Monopoly board for the first example and "three degrees above zero" for the second.

Leaders are also willing to try new problem-solving strategies and are always on the lookout for techniques like "storyboarding," which breaks a problem down into subproblems and then has groups respond to the breakdowns.

The Leader as Team-Builder

To be sure, both divergent and convergent skills are important for leaders. So, too, is a psychological insight into others. In his autobiography, *My American Journey* (New York: Random House, 1995), Colin Powell speaks of having learned what makes American soldiers tick. "They will gripe about being driven to high performance," he reveals. "They will swear they would rather be somewhere else. But at the end of the day, they always ask proudly, 'How'd we do?'"

The leader understands her followers. Like Powell, she knows what makes them tick. And driving them to high performance is a sure way to build a team.

Powell also advises would-be leaders to be skeptical of the experts. While it's fine to listen to them, if you're basing every decision on the advice of others, you may be indirectly under-mining your team. You're expected to have original ideas when you lead and to be willing to fiercely defend them. When the team succeeds in implementing those ideas, the leader works as cheerleader.

The importance of cheerleading extends both to the team as a whole and to its individual components. Consider the story of the conductor of a famous symphony orchestra who was asked which instrument he thought was the most difficult to play. Demonstrating both sensitivity and psychological depth, this leader replied, "Second fiddle." He explained that it was fairly easy to find first violinists, but to find a musician willing to play second fiddle with enthusiasm, that was the challenge. Without second fiddles, of course, there is no harmony.

When you think about your relationship to your team, make certain you treat the first and second fiddlers with equal respect.

The Leader as Manager

Treating workers with respect is now part of the body of man-agement knowledge. The earlier principles of scientific manage-ment may have worked as the old century turned, but they don't work as we enter the new century. Mass production is the aim of only about 25% of the businesses in the country today. Managers' former control over fixed assets has shifted to influ-ence over knowledge workers, so the management skills that worked for earlier generations will not work today.

Management once meant "maintenance." Today that singu-lar word is merged with the leadership thrust: "change." And to effect positive change, the manager-as-leader needs to moti-vate, to turn employees into change agents. She not only helps them better manage the work they're assigned and the work they assign themselves, she also shares strategies with them for better managing the everyday problems that arise from stress, time pressures, energy depletion, emotion, conflict, numerous priorities, poor attitudes, etc.

The Leader as Communicator

Leading is easier for leaders who listen than for leaders who don't. Such leaders ask themselves why people listen and are able to supply a full range of answers. They listen to learn, to show respect, and to demonstrate understanding. They listen to others on a 360° basis; they listen to their inner voice; they listen to what nature tells them.

But leaders do more than listen well. They also speak well, write well, interview well, train others well, and interact with others well.

In terms of speaking, they shun the "sesquipedalian" words, opting for the "little words" that Winston Churchill associated with bigness. They show clarity and conviction when they speak and have mastered sound bites so their words will be remembered. As architects know the strength of triangles, for example, leaders know the strength of "try-angles," motivational phrases that are written as very short inspirational sentences.

Their ability to tell it like it is, without alienating or discouraging followers, is part of the best leaders' personal magnetism. In fact, psychoanalyst Dr. Herbert Freudenberger ties leadership directly to charisma (New York: National Institute of Business Management, "Personal Report for the Executive," July 1, 1988, p. 1). "Charisma," he notes, "is a sense you convey that you are an actual or potential leader, that you can be followed and counted upon."

Your writing and extemporaneous speaking, ideally, convey your leadership talent, too. They'll also reflect your ability to persuade, an important trait for today's leader.

The Leader as Power Distributor

The leaders we admire know how to use power—persuasion power and every other kind as well. They're not afraid of power. They don't worry about being labeled power-hungry. They're not afraid of sharing the power they have. Of course, the ideal leader is using power ethically. She acts with integrity and respects those with whom she interacts, no matter the degree of power they possess themselves.

Leadership sometimes means letting go of power. For example, studies of certain derailed executives reveal their strengths can actually became weaknesses. What had once served them well in their position of authority no longer worked in later circumstances, but they couldn't let go of the strategies they'd come to depend upon.

This unwillingness to change appears, too, in the ineffective style of managers trained in the old school, where authority ruled. Today's employees want a say in the way they do their work. This translates to a sharing of decisions and, by extension, a sharing of power. Managers who refuse to share knowledge, power, decisions, and resources cannot lead for long or cannot lead well if they do.

The Leader as Liaison

Frank Clarke, a retired radio executive from Cincinnati, is one of the best examples you can find of the benefits of liaising (Kevin Johnson, "Three R's, One Man," *USA Today*, July 28, 1992, p. 3A). After seeing the dearth of good books in Southern classrooms, Clarke asked Northern schools to donate old books and desks. In a single three-month period, he managed to send 70,000 used textbooks to impoverished schools, along with much needed office equipment and supplies.

When you fulfill a leadership role by serving in a liaison position, you make connections that benefit everybody. And while your leadership interests may not be of the altruistic variety, there's still much you can do to bridge two or more entities. Remember: "whoso would be a leader must also be a bridge."

The Leader as Planner

Robert L. Dilenschneider, writing in *Sky* magazine ("The Power Clock," April 1993, pp. 20-24), asserts that most leaders know how to handle short-term projects and they've been abundantly instructed on the value of long-range planning. The problem, he feels, is that leaders need help managing their medium-term time for accomplishments two to five years down the road.

He encourages leaders to ask fundamental questions about obstacles, economics, and the "must" of achievement. As you plan for this arguably most critical of ranges, keep the definition of "success" in mind: it's often a question of how you decide to spend your time.

You'll have to put other things aside as you pursue your goal. If you're not single-minded in your purpose, your energies may be dissipated and your cause lost in the process.

Leaders have to simultaneously evince flexibility, for plans do change. If the leader cannot make the mental transitions required to move from one plan to another, she faces failure and a loss of faith on the part of her followers.

Your Action Plan

Now it's time to have the investment you've made in yourself pay off. If you simply put this book on a shelf, now that you've finished reading it, you can't optimize your investment. It takes further work to get a return on it. That work is what your action plan will outline.

Take a few minutes now to formulate a commitment to yourself and to others by answering these questions. Then write a one-paragraph statement of intention. Share it with as many people as you can—this will make you more likely to follow through on it. Keep a record of your progress in order to motivate yourself.

1. Which of the various roles described in the preceding pages is the one you feel least competent playing?
2. What will you do to develop your skills in this area?
3. What most needs doing where you work?
4. What risks are you willing to take?
5. What personal vision, mission, and goal statement can you articulate?
6. Whom can you approach to champion your cause?
7. Whom can you count on to help execute your plans?

8. Which "hats" will you need to wear during the course of this leadership project?
9. What do you need to learn more about?

The Leader as Leader

To the easily discouraged, leadership may seem an overwhelming responsibility. And, in many ways, it is. You have responsibility to your vision, to your team, to your customers, to your organization, to your industry, to your community, and to yourself. You have all kinds of hats to wear and demands upon you. And this is just during *working* hours. Add in the responsibilities you have in your non-professional life and you may start to develop the Superman or Superwoman complex.

No one ever said that leadership would be easy. But you *have* heard it said that leadership is exciting, challenging, and the morally right thing to do. If you've chosen to travel the leadership road, we applaud you. If you've chosen to continue on that path despite the inevitable roadblocks you'll encounter, we salute you. And if you've already effected positive change, we sing your praises.

You're making a difference, an important difference.

Manager's Checklist for Chapter 10

❑ Be a visionary: discover or create your organization's destiny and communicate that vision in ways that inspire followers.

❑ Be a problem-solver: use both divergent and convergent thinking to work on issues that affect individuals, teams, and the organization as a whole, with creativity and courage.

❑ Be a team-builder: bring people together and help them make the most of their individual talents and personalities.

❑ Be a manager—of work, certainly, but also of stress, time, emotions, energy, and people. A good leader is much more than a manager, but to be a leader you must be a good manager.

❏ Be a communicator: listen well, speak well, write well, interview well, train others well, and interact well with others.

❏ Be a power distributor: be confident in using power; share your power, knowledge, decisions, and resources with others; and always be ethical in wielding power.

❏ Be a liaison: form strategic alliances and develop professional bonds through networks.

❏ Be a planner: form operational plans and strategic plans to map out the route to achieve goals and pursue visions.

❏ Be a leader: play a wide range of roles, use diverse skills, adapt according to the situation, and keep in mind your responsibilities to your vision, to your team, to your customers, to your organization, to your industry, to your community, and to yourself.

Index

A

Alliances, forming strategic, 126-129

Armstrong, David M., *Managing by Storying Around*, 40

Arnot, Dr. Bob, *The Biology of Success*, 77

Austin, Nancy, quoted, 18

B

Bacon, Francis, 149

Barton, Bruce, on changing, 70

Benchmarking, explained, 25-27

Berra, Yogi, 100

Big Picture
and mission, 52
seeing, 50-52

Blanchard, Ken, quoted, 9

C

Campbell, Andrew and Goold, Michael, *The Collaborative Enterprise*, 23

Carpenter, Liz, quoted, 96

Castaneda, Carlos, quoted, 130

Change
leader's role, 4
leading change, 14-16
self-assessment, 15-16

Charisma and leadership, 159

Clark, Frank, on liaison, 160

Clausewitz, Karl von, caveat, 148

Cohen, Alan, quoted, 15

Communication
and affiliation, 92-93
and involvement, 92
and loyalty, 89-90
and person expansion, 90-91
and persuasion, 98-100
role in motivation, 89-93
and thinking on your feet, 93-98
and writing, 100-101

Conflict, 60

Consensus
Crawford method for achieving, 63
the Delphi Technique, 61
statements to build, 61-62

Convergent thinking
act aspect, 45
defined, 43-44
fact aspect, 45-46
pact aspect, 44-45
tact aspect, 46-47

Covey, Stephen, quoted, 124

Crane, Frank, quoted, 136

Crawford, C.C., and building consensus, 63

Creativity, in planning, 144

D

Dares, William, as leader, 23
Deming, W. Edwards,
    pride of workmanship, 7
    Plan-Do-Check-Act cycle, 44
Dilenschneider, Robert L., quoted, 160-161
Disney, Walt, quoted, 125
Disraeli, Benjamin, 134
Divergent thinking
    defined, 33-34
    deviation as a method, 34-36
    juxtaposing, 34-35
    incubation as a method, 37-38
    liberation as a method, 41-43
    obviation as a method, 38-41
Donnithorne, Colonel Larry, *The West Point Way of Leadership*, 109-110
Drucker, Peter, 14, 17, 89, 90, 141

E

Einstein, Albert, on human nature, 98
Emerson, Ralph Waldo, quoted, 93
Emotional intelligence, 75
Emotions, tips for managing, 76-77
Empowerment, levels of, 107-108
Energy, tips for managing, 77-79
Ethics
    persuasion and, 98-100
    questions to ask, 28-29
    setting standards, 27-29
Evaluation matrix, explained, 146-147
Evolution, planned, 141

F

Fiedler, Fred, Contingency Theory, 53

Five C's of speech preparation, 88
Flexibility, in partnering relationship, 125
Flowchart, explained, 145-145
Force field analysis, 142
Ford, Henry, and micromanaging, 109
Freudenberger, Herbert, on leadership and charisma, 159

G

Gladstone, William, 134
Goddard, John, and goals, 145
Goethe, quoted, 111
Goleman, Daniel, 75
Ground rules for meetings, 52
Grove, Andy, on workout sessions 94

H

Hayakawa, Samuel I., on victims of culture, 35
Hayes, James, on leadership and communication, 85
Hubbard, Elbert, quoted, 5

I

Iacocca, Lee, on linsting, 93
Imai, Masaaki, *Kaizen*, 139
Intuition, test for, 149-150
Involvement of others, 19

J

"Jelly bean motivation," 91
Juran, Joseph, laguages in organizations, 10

K

Kennedy, John F.
    making a difference, 3
    input from others, 17
K-I-N-D communication technique
    described, 86

example, 87-88
Knowledge sharing
  checklist, 18
  tips for, 111-113
Kotter, John, dynamics of power,
  104, 121

L

Lambert, Jack, on winning, 21
Lao-tzu, defines leadership, 24
Leader
  as a bridge, 125
  as communicator, 85-102, 159
  convergent skills of, 43-47
  defined, 3, 154-155
  divergent skills of, 33-43
  as leader, 162
  as liaison, 124-137, 160
  as manager, 66-84, 158
  as planner. 138-153, 160-161
  as power distributor, 103-123,
    159-160
  as problem-solver, 33-49,
    156-157
  roles of, 3-4
  as team-builder, 50-65, 157-
    158
  traits of, 4-11
  as visionary, 13-32, 155-156
Leadership
  adaptability and, 8
  courage and, 5-7
  defined, 29
  energizing others and, 22-24
  follow through and, 24-25
  influence and, 9-10
  involving others and, 18-20
  multilingual abilities and, 11
  pride and, 7
  sincerity and, 8
  style continuum, 53
  trust factor, 135
  and use of power, 103-104

vulnerability and, 17
Lee, Ivy, 132
Lewin, Kurt
  force-field analysis, 142
  three-step model for change, 13
Listening, as liaison skill, 134
Lombardi, Vince, on dedication, 4
Lord Acton, quoted, 121

M

Machiavelli, Niccolo, *The Prince*,
  106-107, 148
Mailer, Norman, quoted, 37
Manager,
  defined, 1
  roles of, 1-3
Managing
  and eliminating bad habits, 67
  and continuous learning, 82-
    83
  oral communication skills
    and, 85-86
    moving people into, 110-111
  people, 79-82
  stress in, 67-71
  use of time, 72-74
Manipulation, up side of, 10
Martin, Joanne, and Powers,
  Melanie, E., use of anecdotes,
  39
Matsushita, Konosuke, quoted,
  135
Mays, Benjamin Eliah, quoted,
  144-145
McClelland, David, thematic
  apperceptions, 29-30
McDonald's, 20
Meetings, 62-63
"Mental" zone, exercise for, 95
Mentoring, 108-109
Michelangelo and the Sistine
  Chapel, 80

Microsoft, 93
Mindset, creating positive, 111
Mission success, elements, 141-142
Mother Teresa, quoted, 30-31
Motorola, 21
Myers, M. Scott, on motivation, 91

N
Naisbitt, John, *Megatrends*, 113
Napoleon, on sword and mind, 105

P
Patton, General George S., quoted on leading, 7
Pact-Act-Fact-Tact, 44-47
Partnering
    in the community, 128-129
    facets of, 129-130
    in the organization, 127-128
    six C's of, 130-134
    in the workplace, 126-127
Pearson, Christine, on workplace civility, 81-82
"The Penalty of Leadership," 79
People, tips for managing, 81-82
Personal action plan, 161-162
Personality
    flexibility and, 53-54
    and leadership, 53
Persuasion
    characteristics in motivating others, 99-100
    and "denaturing evil," 99-100
Peters, Tom, on weirdos, 98
Peterson, Don, 50
Plan-Do-Check-Act (PDCA), 44
Planned evolution, 141
Plans
    and anticipation of future, 138-139

failure of, 150-151
intuition, use of, 149
long-range, 139-140
medium-range, 141-143
myths about, 143-145
provisos for, 147-149
short-term, 143
tools for, 145-147
Politics
    how to be effective, 114
    influencing unfriendly people
        hyenas, 117-118
        lambs, 116-117
        lions, 118-119
        owls, 116
        queen bees, 119
Powell, Colin, quoted, 22, 157
Power
    defined, 104
    empowerment, 107-108
    force vs. persuasion, 105
    and knowledge, 111-113
    as mutually beneficial process, 105
    politics as part of, 113-120
    praise and, 120
    reference, 121
    struggles, 120-121
Principled Persuasion, 105

R
Reagan, Ronald, as communicator, 100-101
Reich, Robert, on leaders and communication, 85
Revere, Paul, as leader, 23
Rewards
    list of, 58
    teamwork as its own, 59-60
Rigsbee, Ed, *The Art of Partnering*, 128
Russell, Richard, input from others, 16, 17

S

Salk, Jonas, quoted, 36

Schlesinger, Arthur, Jr., quoted, 89, 96

Schopenhauer, Arthur, on truth, 5

Schultz, Howard, quoted, 16

Schwab, Charles, on power of praise, 120

Shaw, George Bernard, quoted, 71, 99

Seidenberg, Tom, on input from employees, 148

Silo-ism, defined, 17

Stack, Jack, *The Great Game of Business*, 11

Stress
and burnout 67-68
causes, 69-70
reducing, 70-71
symptoms, 68-69

Swift, Jonathan, defines vision, 13

T

Taylor, Frederick, management model, 135

Taylor, Herbert J., quoted on ethics, 27

Teams,
aligning tasks and talent, 56-58
characteristics of, 51
commitment of members, 51
conflicts on, 60
expectations for members, 56
high performance, 60-61
keys to successful, 64
maintenance roles on, 54-55
successful meetings of, 62-63
purpose of, 53
task roles on, 54-55

Teamwork, optimal conditions for, 59

Thematic Apperception Test, 29-30

Thinking, convergent, 43-47

Thinking, divergent, 33-43

Thinking on your feet
embedded words and, 95-96
quotations and, 97-98
toss-back definitions and, 96-97

Time
and goal setting, 72
managing, 72-74
questions regarding, 72-73
as relative concept, 74
tips for improving use of, 73-74

Tuckman, Bruce, and form-storm-norm-perform, 59

Tyabji, Hatim, on importance of psychology, 52

V

Violence in the workplace, 74-75

Vision
defined, 13
leaders and vision, 13-32
questions to delineate, 140

W

Wal-Mart, 15

Walton, Sam, on "eliminiating the dumb," 3, 15

Welch, Jack, 1, 37, 93

William H. Mercer, Inc., on relieving stress, 69

Win-win-win, 27 99

WIIFM Factor, 6, 41

Workout sessions, 93-94

Writing, techniques to communicate effectively, 100-101